KW-272-019

PEOPLE FROM THE PAST – No. 1
EDITED BY EGON LARSEN

NINE DAYS' HERO:
Wat Tyler

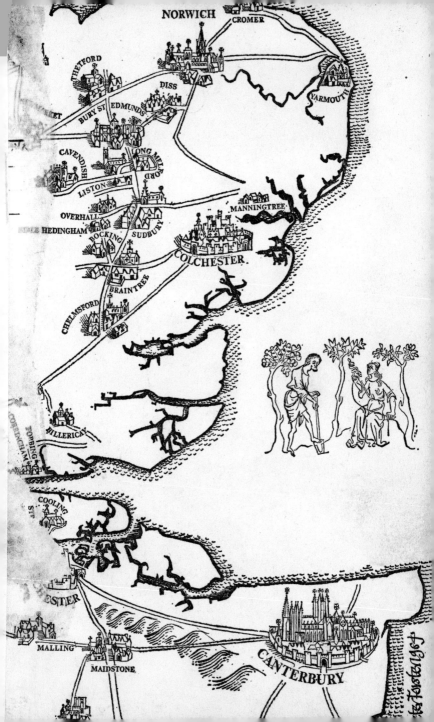

NORWICH

CROMER

THETFORD

DISS

YARMOUTH

BURY ST EDMUNDS

CAVENDISH

LONG MELFORD

LISTON

OVERHALL

MANNINGTREE

HEDINGHAM

BOCKING

SUDBURY

COLCHESTER

BRAINTREE

CHELMSFORD

BILLERICAY

FOBBING

CORRINGHAM

COOLING

STP

ESTER

MALLING

MAIDSTONE

CANTERBURY

F.G. FOSTER 1967

NINE DAYS' HERO:
Wat Tyler

———

JACK LINDSAY

LONDON: DENNIS DOBSON

First published in Great Britain in 1964
by Dobson Books Ltd.
80 Kensington Church Street, London, W.8

This book is copyright under the Berne Convention

© by Jack Lindsay 1964

O 234 777 745

BATTERSEA
PUBLIC LIBRARIES

C 942·038

FYDE

12700

PRINTED IN GREAT BRITAIN BY
C. TINLING AND COMPANY LIMITED
LIVERPOOL, LONDON AND PRESCOT

FOR BERNARD AND JOSEPHINE MILES

600 years ago. The darkness
of desperate and plodding years
breaks open with a campfire-gleam;
the lost and shrouded landscape clears.

Then from the distance of the dust
we hear the call that someone's giving.
The dead, from their eternal moment,
rise up more vivid than the living.

The moment of great hope and love
burns in its irrefutable right.
You know this England, root and branch,
the darkness and the clap of light.

CONTENTS

BATTERSEA
PUBLIC
LIBRARIES

CHAPTER I

HOW IT BEGAN

In the spring of 1381 a commissioner of the poll-tax, Thomas Bampton, rode out from London to Brentwood in Essex. His task was to revise the taxation-returns for the hundred of Barstaple; for those returns, like practically all the returns sent in from anywhere in England, were suspected to be falsified. He had with him three clerks and two serjeants-at-arms, and did not feel there was any particular danger in what he was to do. In large numbers of other places there were more commissioners at work trying to get in correct returns.

Bampton began his inquiry on 30 May and ordered the folk of the marshland villages of Fobbing, Corringham, and Stanford-le-Hope to appear before him. His order was obeyed, but not in the spirit in which he had meant it to be taken. The sturdy peasants and fishermen of Fobbing turned up to a man, but with arms in their hands, and they refused flatly to pay a penny more. Thomas Baker, their spokesman, was so downright and defiant that Bampton commanded the serjeants to arrest him. At once about 100 men attacked the official party, throwing stones and driving them out of Brentwood.

Bampton, the steward of a powerful lord, was astounded. He hurried back to report his mishap to the King's

Council. But the councillors were still unable to realize the strength of the people's anger against the poll-tax, which amounted to 1s. a head on everyone over fifteen. They decided that the riot must have been a chance outburst and that the offenders could easily be cornered and dealt with as an example to other murmurers. They dispatched to Brentwood an important official, Sir Robert Belknap, the chief justice of the common pleas, but they gave him only a small retinue for the work of seeking out and punishing the rioters.

Great Seal of Richard II.

But the men of Fobbing and Corringham had not been standing idle. They felt that the only way to safeguard themselves was to worsen their offence and to make their defiance general. They took to the woods and sent messengers all round south Essex with the call that the hour for action had now come. Two men of Rainham, as well as two London butchers, went galloping through the countryside, assuring everybody that the commons of London and Kent would stand by their fellows of Essex in any fight. The labourers and fishermen who had flung the stones at Brentwood had understood the temper of the mass of the people better than the councillors issuing instructions in London. They knew that if the call were given, the people would rally against the King's Council and all the officials connected with the tax.

All around, men began sharpening their axes and knives, testing their longbows, searching out any old bit of armour, or gathering billhooks, scythes, sickles, spears. Large bands collected at Brentwood, Baddow, and near Colchester. And perhaps flares from Fobbing, a haunt of hardy smugglers that looked down on the mudflats of the Thames, sent signals across to Cooling in Kent; for there were many men in Kent, as in Essex, waiting impatiently for a signal to rise, and the tumults began there fast on the heels of those around Brentwood.

Before Belknap had started summoning jurors to present indictments against the rioters, a rebellion was under way.

As soon as he arrived, he was seized by a host of men who made him swear on the Bible never again to hold such a session or act as a justice in such inquests. Then, after extracting from him a list of the local justices who had convicted tax-defaulters, his captors let him return to London. But they held his three clerks, who were found to be the ones who had also come with Bampton. Considering that their reappearance proved them to be settled enemies of the people, they beheaded them as traitors. They then inflicted the same fate on three of the jurors who were tracked down. The heads of the six men were set on poles and carried through Brentwood and the neighbouring villages as demonstrations of the rebellious course from which there could now be no turning back.

11

News of the uprising spread rapidly through all Essex. In the fields and the lanes, the market-places and the churchyards, the peasants put their heads together and muttered. Then they came together in bands and shouted their determination to refuse the tax, to refuse all the demands which they considered unjust and oppressive. Brandishing their scythes and hooks, they attacked the landlords and the other men whom they had marked down as inveterate enemies. Taking charge of their own small area, they waited for a call that would draw them into a wider field of action.

Kent too was already in tumult. By 2 June a small armed group under Abel Ker of Erith burst into the monastery of Lesness and made the abbot take an oath to support them. Probably they used the form that was to become general: 'For King Richard and the True Commons.' Abel and his men then took a boat across the Thames and conferred with Essex leaders near Barking.

River-Fishing.   (From Harleian MS. No. 4374.)

They returned to Kent on the 4th, bringing with them reinforcements of 100 fighters. They marched on the town of Deptford, where the folk were already astir. Abel put himself under the masterbaker Robert Cave, who was in charge there. A council was held and plans drawn up. The rebels issued a proclamation that 'none which are dwelling within twelve miles of the sea should go with them, but keep the coast of the sea from enemies'. The proclamation also stated that there were more kings than one in the land—a hit at the unpopular John of Gaunt, who was considered to control his young nephew the King. This, the rebels said, they would not allow; they would have no king but Richard II.

The rebels feared, we see, that the French might take advantage of the risings and attempt an invasion. (In fact, four years later, when the revolt was long over, there was call to arms in London in view of a French threat.) The way in which the rebels took such careful thought as to the consequences of their actions is one of many details which show what a responsible attitude they tried to maintain and how thorough were their considerations.

At Rochester, the Kentish contingent found men from Gravesend gathered, talking of an injustice done to an inhabitant of their town. On Whit Monday, 3 June, an agent of Sir Simon Burley had come with two serjeants and tried to arrest a citizen, Robert Belling, as an escaped bondsman. This was an affront to the town's privileges, since Belling had long been living there. Burley, who was not in England at the time, was hated as one of the courtiers thought to be misleading the King, 'a naughty man, and one contemptuous of the lowborn'. His agent demanded what was then the huge sum of £300 for Belling's release; and when the citizens refused to pay, he had the arrested man bound and carried to Rochester Castle.

The band under Cave agreed to help the Gravesend men in rescuing Belling. More detachments joined in; and after a day of assaults upon the castle, the constable of the keep surrendered. The attackers broke open the dungeons and released the prisoners, who were mostly men sentenced for infringements of the Statute of Labourers or for evasions of the poll-tax.

Now several thousand strong, the rebels marched up the Medway to Maidstone, which since the 7th had been held by the people. All the way they destroyed tax-records, indeed any legal documents. This sort of destruction went on all through the rebellion. The peasants burned or tore up all records of servitude in every manor house, all court-rolls and bailiff-accounts in which were set out their labour-dues and obligations of service to the lords.

At Maidstone they executed a rich burgess, John Southall, whom they denounced as a traitor; and they made the town their headquarters. For here were the two men who played the leading part in organizing and inspiring the revolt, Wat Tyler and John Ball. Ball, a priest, was in the jail, from which he was set free by 20,000 men, as he had prophesied when sentenced by Archbishop Simon of Sudbury.

While Rochester Castle was being taken by storm, fighting had broken out elsewhere in the county. Outside Canterbury, rebels attacked the financier John Legge, who was specially hated as the initiator of the poll-tax. After a short combat he took to flight. The rebels then turned to a manor house belonging to Robert Hales, the King's treasurer, who was also Prior of the Order of St. John of Jerusalem—in which character he held the manor.

Storming a Fort. (Harleian MS. 4379.)

The building was ransacked and all manorial records went up in flames.

Now we can pause to look at Wat Tyler. About his earlier life we know very little. He has often been confused with a John Tyler, who appears for the first time in the chronicle of Stow, who wrote under Queen Elizabeth I. This John, we learn, was at work tiling a house in Dartford, when he heard that the tax-collectors had called at his place and insulted his daughter. He caught up a lathing-stick and ran boisterously home, where he started arguing with the collector. 'The collector,' says Stow, 'answered with stout words and strake at the tyler;

whereupon the tyler, avoiding the blow, smote the collector with the lathing-staff that the brains flew out of his head. Whereupon great noise arose in the street, and the poor people being glad, everyone prepared to support the said John Tyler.'

But this John was certainly not our Wat. The juries of two places near Maidstone, later, both called Wat 'of Essex', and a Maidstone document styled him, 'Walter Tyler of Colchester.' John Ball also came from Colchester, so that it is likely they had long known one another and that the fiery preacher had influenced Tyler's outlook.

Tyler may have been a tiler by profession—or his name may have merely meant that his father or grandfather had worked at tiling. Thus the tax-rolls of 1381 for Sible Hedingham in north Essex mention three John Tylers and one Henry Tyler among the tenants, together with a John Tyler who is actually a tiler. Names at this time might come from all sorts of chance-matters. You might be called after your craft or your place of birth: the Duke of Lancaster was John of Gaunt or Ghent, named after the town where he had been born. You might be called after the site of your house, after your trade-sign, or after a mere nickname. One account of the period does cite Wat as 'Walter Helyere (roofer) or Tyler', and another calls him *unus tegulator*, 'a certain tiler'. But the men penning these descriptions may have merely been guessing from his name.

Tilers must have been numerous, for the towns provided them with much work. Thatch was inflammable, and London had a law that tiles must be used—though, like many medieval laws, it was not very well observed. But tiling was a fairly humble profession and the Tilers'

Company was a lesser one—not formally organized till 1536, like the Bricklayers'. Many tilers took part in the revolt; and another Walter Tyler was a local leader in Norfolk.

A later chronicler, Grafton, tells us that our Wat was living in his early life, apparently as an apprentice, with Richard Lyons, a lapidary and wine-merchant of London, who 'on a tyme did beate him'. Lyons was a swindling financier of the kind that in these years had been stirring the people's wrath; and he served for some time in the French wars as serjeant of Edward III. He had been a money-lender to the King and had raised subsidies for him. In 1376 Parliament impeached him for many frauds and cheats, and he was deprived of his lands and goods—though he managed to get these back through influential supporters. For 1379-80 he seems to have sat in Parliament for Essex.

He was thus the sort of person that Wat Tyler and his men most disliked; and it is of much interest that Wat may well have served under him in France in some capacity, and there have fallen foul of him. (The chronicler, Froissart, states that Wat had fought in France.) The conflict with Lyons may have started Wat thinking along the lines that led him at last to become a resolute rebel, and his evident knowledge of army matters can only have been gained abroad in the French wars where so many English commoners had seen service.

All we can be sure about Wat, then, is that he came of a family of craftsmen, that he was a native of Colchester, and that he had served in the French wars. We may add the probability that two persons in different ways had had a strong effect on him—on the one hand, John Ball,

Siege of a Town.

whose preachings of rebellious brotherhood and equality
we shall later examine; and on the other hand, Richard
Lyons, with whom Wat had come into collision and who
stood out for him as an example of all that was most corrupt and tyrannical in the world of the time.

Why was Wat at Maidstone? Revolt had first broken
out in his native Essex, where Colchester was soon involved. We should have expected him to take the lead
in his own county. Some accident, however, of business
may have taken him into Kent and he may have been
caught there when the revolt occurred. But when we
consider his ardent character and also the fact that the
revolt could have been no surprise to him, we may
suggest that it is more likely he had gone deliberately
into Kent so as to be near John Ball's prison and to ensure
his liberation at the earliest possible moment. If we can

call any one man the architect of the revolt, it was Ball, who had long broadcast his revolutionary message; and if there had been general agreement among leaders of the people that a revolt was necessary and Wat Tyler was the best man to take over the military command, it was natural that Wat should want to take action from the outset with John Ball at his side.

But if the past years are shrouded in doubt and uncertainty, from this moment Wat Tyler is in the full light of history till his death. He had only nine days left to him, but in those nine days he shook England and showed himself a leader with remarkable powers of organization and strategy, able to discipline and control his hastily-gathered army of peasants and craftsmen. Even the monks who wrote the chronicles of the period and who were bitterly opposed to the rebels in every respect, paid him reluctant tributes, admitting that he was a 'crafty fellow of an excellent wit, though lacking grace'. or that 'he was endowed with great intelligence if only it had been applied to a rightful purpose'.

During the nine days when in effect he was ruler of England, there was never a single questioning of his command by anyone in the rebel ranks; his hold on their loyalties never slackened. Even when he issued orders for looters to be hanged, he was instantly obeyed. The speed and completeness with which he was elected to take charge of the rebel forces further argues that he was well known at least to the leading men of the discontented localities, and that a considerable amount of preparation had gone on before the outbreak at Brentwood.

During the revolt the rebels, especially in Norfolk, often spoke of belonging to a Great Society. This term, however, seems to express the sense they had of being bound together in a great and adventurous brotherhood rather than to define any definite underground organization. But there had certainly for many years been an exchange of rebellious ideas, in which the carriers were wandering craftsmen, religious beggars, vagrants, and all sorts of broken men who roved around. And in the various localities the peasants had long shown their capacity to come together in what were called 'conventicles', groups suddenly organized for resistance to demands that were felt as intolerable. Each locality no doubt had its recognized strong characters or leaders, to whom grievances were brought—though only in moments of sharp struggle did the conventicle and its leaders come into the sight of the manor lords.

But now the struggle was abruptly out in the open, over increasingly wide areas of England. On 7 June the rebels of Kent chose Wat Tyler 'to maintain them and act as their counsellor'. And after that the men of the other areas, whether converging on London or getting into contact with the main bodies of revolt, always accepted him as the supreme commander.

CHAPTER 2

WHY THE COMMONS REVOLTED

BUT before we go on with the story of the revolt, we must know more of the reasons for the sudden and general uprising of the people. The immediate cause, as we saw, was the poll-tax. When the young King, Richard, had come to the throne in 1377, the Government's finances had been in a bad way; and his councillors considered that the only way to raise the needed supplies was to find a new method of extracting yet more money from the peasants. The Northampton Parliament of 1380 voted for a poll-tax—that is, a flat tax levied per head of population. A poll-tax had been imposed three years before; but the new one was three times as heavy, and though there was a pretence of rich men having to provide relief for poor neighbours, in fact the burden fell solidly on peasant and craftsman. A poem of the period, in French and Latin makes the point that the ones who felt the weight of taxation were the poor, especially as the collectors were liable to embezzle the money they got in. It adds:

Now folk can't give a penny more,
as you may judge from their sighs.

21

> I think if only they found a leader,
> in revolt they'd rise.

The sum demanded was 1s. from every adult. Parliament made no disguise of the aims of the tax, and to justify the effort to get the money out of the lower classes, it declared, 'all the wealth of England has gone into the hands of labourers and workers'. In many areas the poorest folk had to find the whole sum.

When the collectors tried to get the tax in, the returns were falsified wholesale. Whereas in 1377, 1,355,201 persons had paid, now only 896,481 (excluding the palatinates of Durham and Chester) were found on the rolls. In some areas the population had apparently fallen by 50 per cent, in none by less than 20 per cent. It seems that what men had done was to omit all female dependents other than a wife; most villages thus showed a large excess of males and some showed no unmarried women, no dependents at all.

The collectors had been charged to pay in two-thirds of their receipts in January, the remaining third in June 1381; and as soon as the accounts came in, the Government grew alarmed. On 22 February it demanded the immediate collection of the total sum due, and on 16 March it added that there was clear evidence of the collectors and the constables acting negligently and corruptly. So fresh commissioners were to go into the shires, make more correct lists of the people liable to tax, and jail all who resisted. John Legge, whom we saw the men of Kent attacking, was said to have suggested these steps.

Many of the persons nominated refused to serve, and the Government's orders were carried out with much difficulty. The second roll was drawn up by March. In many regions almost every family had made false returns and was therefore open to fresh charges and to punishment. The commissioners were hard at work in April and May. In Suffolk some 13,000 omitted names were collected in a few weeks; in Norfolk, some 8,000. But in the midst of the work of revised collection there came the outburst.

But though the discontent over the poll-tax had been the spark that caused the explosion, the poll-tax alone could never have brought about such drastic results. To understand the rebellion we must have some idea of the medieval world into which Wat Tyler and the others had been born, and of the direction in which the world had been moving in the fourteenth century.

First and foremost, this world was a feudal world. That is, it was based on a class of peasants who were tied to the soil under the lords who held the land, while the lords themselves were graded in a system of varying grandeurs —the lesser ones bound in service to the greater, with the King as the supreme feudal lord. The tied-down peasant was a serf or villein. He was the head of a family, and was almost always linked with other peasants in the community of a village or hamlet. Usually he had his own small crop-land in the village area, with a share in the group-rights of grazing and of access to the communal woodland.

The lord, who stood over the peasant, charged him a rent: which in effect meant that he took for himself the surplus of the serf's production—all that the latter produced above a living subsistence. And mostly he took it by a sheer show of force. The rent might be computed

Two-wheeled Plough. (From Harleian MS. No 4374.)

as a fixed or changing proportion of the things that the serf produced on his holding—grain, dairy products, stock. Or it might take the form of forced labour that the serf put in on the lord's own special land, his demesne.

As society had grown richer and more complicated, as markets grew and there was more money in circulation, labour services and rents-in-kind (rents paid in produce and not in money) were often turned or commuted into money-rents. But the system was still at root the same. The money represented in a different form the same extorted surplus. In the earlier phase lasting from the tenth to the twelfth century, as the State with its King's law was still comparatively slight and undeveloped in structure, the payment of the feudal rents was mainly carried out under the local or manorial Courts which were completely dominated by the lord himself.

Towns had long been growing up as centres of trade and handicraft; and they sought to win freedom from feudal dues and burdens by gaining charters from the King or buying themselves out of the grip of the lords. Mostly they traded only in things that had been locally produced, though a few places like London imported goods (such as spices and wines) from abroad. Their own workshops were generally small, run by a master-craftsman with one or two apprentices or journeymen (called valets, yeomen, or serving-men in the fourteenth century: fully-trained craftsmen who lacked the resources to set up as masters). Only a few industries, above all cloth-making, were linked with a wide market inside England and reaching to the Continent. In these the big merchants mustered large groups of craftsmen; but they acted as middlemen more than as organizers of production such as we find much later in the first forms of the factory-system.

The town craftsmen were gathered together in gilds —masters, journeymen, and apprentices. In the original scheme the apprentice became a journeyman, who in time became a master, and there was thus a unity of interest in the gild; but when the majority of journeymen could no longer hope to become independent masters, that unity broke up. The masters, however, wanted to keep everyone in the gild, so as to control and if necessary suppress the dependent craftsmen. When the journeymen tried to set up their own organizations, the masters put them down or brought them into line with their own system. Thus, the masters in 1306 suppressed the effort of the journeymen shoemakers of London to set up their own body; the cloth shearers in 1350 complained of combinations among the men against the masters. These attempts of the journeymen to assert themselves were to grow much stronger in the next century.

At the moment the main struggle in the large towns was between the rich merchant gilds that wanted to monopolize the sale of manufactured goods, and the craftsmen gilds that were fighting against the merchants' schemes for fixing prices and controlling output.

Tournament. (Harleian MS. 4379.)

Now let us look back at the land. The great lords or landowners, who were close to the King and did much in shaping his policy, had estates scattered over many counties. From time to time conflicts arose among them, which could swell until they affected the whole country. Then the King had to take one side and the other side became a sort of Opposition party. As the greatest magnate, the King had his supremacy, but he could not stand aside from, and above, the really big disputes of the other magnates. The smaller barons found themselves on one side or another for various reasons—because of the terms of their land-holding, their marriage connexions, their need to keep in with the great man of their area.

The lowest rank among the feudal lords was that of the knights. Originally they owed military service to the King's host, being included in the quota of mounted men for which the barons were liable. In return a knight got one or two manors and did the routine work of local administration for the royal Government. He might be little more than a rich freeholder, drawing £20 or £30 a year from a small manor, or he might draw four or five times as much and come close in importance to the lowest baronial levels. But, until the sixteenth and seventeenth centuries, the knights were controlled by the barons and showed no political independence.

The lords of the great estates ruled England, and their estates were the chief factor in the economic situation. So it is to those estates that we must look for the explanation of the revolt that Wat Tyler led.

They lay all over England, but the most important regions were the south and south-east. Hence the way in which Kent, Essex, and East Anglia were the furious centres of the revolt. But even here there were many small lords with one to five manors, and free tenants who owed their lord only slight service or rent for their land. Still, smallholders often were driven by poverty to sell their labour cheaply to the big estates, especially at harvest-time. The poet Langland depicts them cramped for room on their plots and intruding on the strip of the next man:

If I plant or plough, I pinch so narrowly
that I fetch a furrow or a foot's swathing

from my next neighbour and gnaw his half-acre.
If I reap, I overreach, or tell the reaper privately
to seize for me with his sickle what was sown by
another.

Reaping and Gleaning.

In the north and north-west conditions were much less
feudally developed, particularly in areas where only
sheep and cattle grazed. But the great estate was the
typical medieval form and in many parts of England controlled the lives of all the inhabitants.

The main unit was the manor. This generally consisted
of the home farm or demesne, with anything up to 100
or 500 acres of crop-land; of the smaller holdings of free
or enserfed peasant tenants, 10 or 30 acres—not to mention the acre plots of smallholders or cottagers; and of
the woods, wastes, and pastures held in common by the
villagers. Often manor and village coincided, but at
times a village was cut up among two or more manors
or a manor took in several villages or hamlets.

The manor was run by the lord's bailiff, who had under him a peasant reeve, a sort of foreman, ostensibly chosen by the folk but invariably siding with the lord. Chaucer gives a picture of his shrewd capacity:

The yielding of his seed, and of his grain,
His lord's sheep, his *neet*, his dairy,   (*cattle*)
His swine, his horse, his *stoor*, and his poultry   (*stock*)
Was wholly in this reeve's governing . . .
There was no bailiff, nor *herd*, nor other hind
                                        (*shepherd*)
That he not knew his sleight and his *covyn;*   (*deceit*)
They were adread of him, as of the death.
His dwelling was full fair upon a heath,
With green trees i-shadowed was his place.
He could better than his lord purchase.
Full rich he was a-stored privily,
His lord well could he please subtly . . .

Labour on the demesne was mainly unpaid, carried out by the tenants as rent-services. They did the ploughing, reaping, and carting, though there would also be permanent hired men as well as casual labour taken on at such times as harvest. The bailiff or the reeve had to get the largest yield possible from demesne, collect the rents that were paid in money or kind, discipline and fine the tenants in the manor court (under the supervision of a higher official, the steward), and sell the surplus produce at the best price in the local market.

The estate was run by a host of officials, each of whom had his own niche of authority and over whom stood the lord's council composed of the local gentry, lawyers,

B

Male Costume, time of Edward III. (Royal MS.
19 D. ii., and Strutt.)

and land agents. The expansion of the manorial system, which had led to this position, had begun in the eleventh century and in England had reached its height in the thirteenth and fourteenth. (In France and West Germany the best days had come more than a century earlier.) By the time of Richard II the organization was growing too complicated and top-heavy; but instead of halting this development, the lords went on making it worse.

They had taken to making surveys of their lands and to keeping yearly accounts as well as records of the manorial Courts. As the produce from the soil and handicraft industry grew larger in volume, the population grew. Trade too went on swelling, both inside the country and between England and the Continent. Prices rose. The lords through their agents and officials, did all they could to continue the increase in production and to sell more and more of the produce in the market.

But even if they had found effective ways of putting some of the profit back into the land, they mostly were not interested in such a procedure. They did their utmost to get as much as possible of the new wealth for themselves. Their taste for luxury was growing all the while, and the increased demand for finery led the chroniclers to denounce the new fashions. About 1345 one declares that the 'old honest and good usage' is ended; men wear strait-waisted clothes with all sorts of decorations and sashes, 'with sleeves and tippets of surcoats and hoods overlong and large and overmuch hanging, so that, if I tell the truth, they were more like to devils and

Male Costume, time of Richard II.
(Royal MS. 20 B. vi., and Harleian MS. 1319.)

tormentors in their clothing and shoeing and other array than to men'. In 1362 we are told that 'wearers of such attire ought to be considered players and worthless fellows rather than barons, actors rather than knights, buf-

31

foons rather than squires. They are lions in the hall and hares in the field'. In 1365, 'the monstrosity and tightness of these garments did not permit them to kneel to God or to the saints or do reverence to their lords or to help themselves without great discomfort; how many indeed put them to the test in hostile combat?'

Yet all the while, with the administration of the manors growing more complicated and costly, and the need of ready money for the lords' personal expenditure more acute, the Government was demanding more and more taxes, in part to meet the charges of the wars.

How then were the lords to deal with such a situation? They struggled to go on expanding incomes by expanding estates—by clearing forests or draining marshes. All such extension of the cultivated area was a valuable service. But it had its limits. And so the lords also tried to wring extra services out of their peasants. Then, when no more services could possibly be extracted, they started increasing the rents in kind or money. At times their officials showed much ingenuity in reorganizing the estates and finding new ways of bringing in more profits. The most efficient and hard-driving landlords were often the great monasteries, where the increase in wealth further led to a decay of the active spirit among the monks. The monks then found no attraction in manual labour and employed large numbers of lay brothers for all menial or heavy jobs. But though much shrewdness was shown by the landlords, secular or ecclesiastical, in finding devices for raising more income, no thought was given to any deepgoing ways of changing the methods of work in agriculture or handicraft. All the effort was put into finding more land, not into making better use of what was already cultivated; into getting more out of the peasant, not into finding ways whereby, individually or in his group, he might become more productive. As a result there was not even any general increase in the average yield of grain per acre.

With the fourteenth century the system had thus reached its limit of expansion. Unable to expand more, it began to contract, to decline. The prices of the produce from the land went down. Markets shrank. And there was a rise in the prices of various commodities (which included tools and the like, and so made up part of the costs of working the land). This sort of thing was not new, but the force with which it now asserted itself was both new and disturbing. And all the while the lords felt their sources of income threatened, they saw the overhead expenses on their estates growing heavier.

To make things worse for them, they had to struggle with a shortage of both serfs and free labourers. The expansion of the thirteenth century had brought about an increase in population, but the economy had not developed as fast, and so the supply of food was inadequate. Malnutrition became widespread. When crops failed, there was a famine, and in such conditions of worsened health plagues and all sorts of diseases were sure to appear and play havoc. There was a plague in 1315-16 and in 1348-9 came a terrible bubonic plague, called the Black Death. Famines too were always threatening. Nine years after Wat Tyler's revolt there was 'great want' all over England. 'You would see infants and children, in highways and houses, wailing and clamouring on account of hunger, begging for bread, nor was the mother able to help them.'

Inviting to the Repast. (Royal MS. 14 E. 3.)

Coming on top of the other setbacks, the Black Death had a profound social effect. In many places a half to three-quarters of the population died; and in a few places there was complete extermination. But even where the effects were comparatively light, the shortage of tenants and labourers was made worse. The lords and their officials racked their wits to use every trick that could tie men down or draw them in. Sometimes they cancelled the agreements they had made for commuting labour services into money. Sometimes they had to resort to sheer force. But in many areas they had holdings which they couldn't fill by any legal device or violent pressure.

Thus the Black Death brought to a head the various factors making for the decline of the feudal manor in England. It did not create the crisis, but sharpened it. The unsettling effect of the increased use and need of money in a world built on the notion of interlocked ser-

34

vices is seen in songs of the period and of the following
years. Thus 'Sir Penny' is hymned:

> On earth it is a little thing
> And reigns as a rich king,
> Where he is lent in land.
> Sir Penny is his name called,
> He makes both young and old
> Bow unto his hand.
>
> Popes, kings, and emperors,
> Bishops, abbots, and priors,
> Parsons, priest, and knight,
> Dukes, earls, and each baron,
> To serve him they are full *boon*   (*eager*)
> Both by day and night.
>
> He may buy both heaven and hell,
> And each thing that is to sell,
> On earth he has such grace.
> He may loose and he may bind,
> The poor are aye put behind
> Where he comes in place.

CHAPTER 3

A LAND OF PEASANTS

THE lords found themselves in increasing difficulties. The tenants and labourers were not so easy to coerce, and even what produce they got from the demesne was harder to sell at a good profit. They began to lease out the demesne, with all the beasts, implements, and plant for working it. In this situation they did not need serfs so so much as they had done, and so were ready to commute ploughing services and the like for a money payment. Some lords took the way out of ceasing to grow crops on the demesne and throwing it open to sheep. Thus began the development which in the next couple of centuries was going to wipe out a large number of villages and raise the loud complaints that 'sheep were eating up men'.

In the areas where the lords were doing their best to get money in by commuting services, the serfs had to find money in place of the forced labour they had been giving. The better-off peasants were pleased at this change, but the poorer ones often found that it made life yet more difficult. The poet Langland draws a vivid picture of their hardships.

. . . the poor in the cottage

charged with a crew of children and with a land-
lord's rent.
What they win by their spinning to make their
porridge with,
milk and meal, to satisfy the babes,
the babes that continually cry for food,
this they must spend on the rent of their houses,
aye, and themselves suffer with hunger,
with woe in winter rising a-nights,
in the narrow room to rock the cradle,
carding, combing, clouting, washing, rubbing,
  winding, peeling rushes,
pitiful it is to read the cottage woman's woe,
aye, and many another that puts a good face on it,
ashamed to beg, ashamed to let the neighbours know
all that they need, noontide and evening.
Many the children and nought but a man's hands
to clothe and feed them; and few pennies come in,
and many mouths to eat the pennies up.
Bread and thin ale for them are a banquet,
cold flesh and cold fish are like roast venison.
A farthingworth of mussels, a farthingworth of
cockles,
were a feast to them on Fridays or fastdays,
it were a charity to help these, that be at heavy
charges.

In areas where the markets were weakest and there
was the least stimulus to produce things for sale, the
practice of leasing out the demesne was more attractive
than that of cultivating it by forced labour. That was the
easiest way for them to raise ready cash. But in the south

37

Bird-catching by Clap-net.

and south-east were the richest and most advanced areas. There towns were thickest and good ports were easy to reach, while industry was growing up in the countryside. So the lords were more easily able to work out ways of marketing their produce and even to think of markets overseas. They were in consequence more reluctant to lease out the demesne and they tried hard to cling to their rights of forcing the peasants to work for them without wages.

Not that any area had a uniform tendency. The letting-out of manors is often found in Norfolk, a rich area; and generally in any single village the peasants were growing ever more unequal in their fortunes. Some rose up the scale and bought a fair amount of land; others were still working as serfs; yet others found it difficult to keep alive at all. The towns too had often very different fates. In some East Anglian towns there was a busy trade and manufacture; in others like Bury a heavy hand of lordship held them back.

The shortage of labour hit the lesser nobles and knights hard, for they had smaller numbers of serfs as tenants and had always been more dependent on hiring cottagers at harvest-time. For a while, the Black Death, helping to bring about a sharp rise in both prices and wages, created something like chaos. Serfs ran from the manors to which they were legally bound, and joined the ranks of landless men and smallholders working for wages. As they had no stake in the land, they had little or nothing to lose: and if they managed to stay uncaught for a year in a town, they lost their serf-status.

The lords and manorial officials were at their wits' end. Some magnates took to kidnapping or luring serfs away from the smaller landlords, who had no recourse against them. The serfs themselves at times acquiesced in such changes, as life was likely to be easier on an estate belonging to the King or one of the great nobles, who

A Parliament of the time of Henry V. (Harleian MS. No. 2278.)

39

was not personally present, than under an efficient and exacting monastery.

In June 1349, less than a year after the first outbreak of the Black Death, the Government issued an Ordinance of Labourers, which was soon strengthened by parliamentary Statutes. The central machinery of the State had been growing more effective since the thirteenth century, so that now it was becoming possible to enforce such regulations; and the need to enforce them led in turn to a firmer grounding of the governmental system with its central controls. The Statute of Labourers thus marked an important moment in the growth of the State, which could now attempt to do what had previously been carried out by the local gentry or nobles through their personal officials. This point explains why the men led by Wat Tyler were particularly exasperated against the big State-officials who had directed the poll-tax.

The aim of the Statute was to provide cheap labour and to prevent the Commons from using their strong position which had come about through the shortage of workers on the land. All men and women under the age of sixty, who did not own enough land to take up all their time, were ordered to accept any job offered to them, at rates estimated at the lowest average (2d. to 3d. a day, not 3d to 4d.) prevailing in 1347, or at certain rates fixed for some particular occupations. A man had to give his own lord the first refusal of his services; and only contracts for a year or six months were recognized, contracts by the day were forbidden. The lord's word, without any other proof, was held sufficient to establish the existence of a contract and its terms. His officials and the local gentry could clap any defaulter into the stocks. Justices, chosen from the local nobles and gentry, were appointed to try delinquents at the quarter-sessions, and to fine or imprison them. Naturally they almost always imposed a fine, since that brought in money, while to jail a man was to lose his labour.

For six years after the Black Death the profits of the sessions went to lighten the taxation assessments of the districts. So the gentry, as the main tax-payers, had every reason to enforce the law thoroughly and to fine as many peasants as possible. The justices had their salaries paid out of the fines. In three years the workers paid in about £10,000 in fines, to the tax-relief of the rich. In some places they paid in more than the sum total of the taxes. Between 1349-77 some 9,000 cases were tried, and in almost every one of them the employer won. To increase the terrors of the Statute, branding with red-hot irons and outlawry were added as sanctions.

In addition a Statute of 1361 gave the justices powers against all persons troubling the peace or who went wandering and refused to 'work as they were wont to do before this time'.

No minimum had been mentioned for wages and little effort seems to have been put into keeping prices down to the vaguely-stated 'reasonable' level.

All these measures, however, did not cow the people, who began to fight back. Hence the strengthening of the justices' powers against rioters and 'evil doers'. The peasants took advantage of the dire need of their labour to run away from strict lords. The Commons at the Parliament of 1376 reported that if 'their masters reprove them for bad service, or offer to pay them for the said service according to the form of the said statutes, they

Shooting at Butts. (Royal MS., 19, c. viii.)

fly and run away out of their service and out of their own country, from County to County and town to town, in strange places unknown to their said masters'.

The next year Parliament expressed alarm at the widespread movements among the peasants aimed at the ending of serfdom. The peasants had somehow heard of the great survey 'Domesday Book', drawn up by William the Conqueror, and they kept appealing to it for proof that their particular locality had had freemen and not serfs at that time: 'They affirm that they are quite and utterly discharged of all manner of serfdom due whether of their own bodies of their tenure, and will not suffer distresses to be levied on them, but menace the servants of their lords in life and members, and what is more, they draw together in great bands, and bind themselves in confederation that each shall aid the others and bind themselves in confederation that each shall aid the others to constrain their lords by the strong hand.'

Thus we find the charge that in 1380 at Strixton in Northamptonshire, on the eve of the general revolt, they 'confederated themselves in conventicles and took an oath to resist lord and bailiff, and to refuse their due custom and service'.

There were many complaints at the insolence of the labourers, who in some areas were able to raise their standard of living. Thus the poet Gower, writing in Anglo-French, echoes the talk of the landlords in 1375: 'The world goes fast from bad to worse, when shepherd and cowherd for their part demand more for their labour than the master-bailiff was wont to take in days gone by. Labour is now at so high a price that he who will order his business aright must pay 5s. or 6s. for what cost 2s. in former times. Labourers of old were not wont to eat of wheaten bread; their meat was of beans or coarser corn, and their drink was of water alone. Cheese and milk were a feast to them, and rarely ate they of other dainties; their dress was of hodden grey; then the world was ordered aright for folk of this sort.' We see that despite all the penalties some landlords were ready to pay illegally high rates to get the labour that they desperately needed.

Another cause of trouble lay in the fact that the rich peasants did not at all like the way in which the lords, who often still had many enserfed labourers, kept on trying to force on to their fields all the free workers at a very low wage and to eliminate competition. They, and the lesser gentry, lacked the power to use force to get hold of workers; and if they paid illegally high wages, as they did at times, they were liable to be prosecuted. So they grew more and more hostile to the nobles of their area, and many of them joined the revolt under Wat Tyler.

The way in which villages had been growing socially divided for some centuries were thus of much importance in creating the strains and stresses that led to the great revolt. The better-off class was that of the yardlanders and half-yardlanders; their 'yard' being the quarter-hide or 'virgate' that had become the normal holding of the villein. Below them were smallholders, free or enserfed, some owning an acre or two in the common fields, others owning no more than a cottage and squatting rights on the wasteland. But by 1381 a class of rich peasants had risen up. We find four or five families in a village with 60 to 100 acres of crop-land and some hundreds of livestock. Some yardlanders still existed, and below them were the mass of landless labourers.

The way in which the peasants had taken to selling their produce in the local markets had had much to do with this growth of a few rich men, who had taken advantage of the situation and whose rise had meant the loss of land by large numbers of others. True, the markets were growing slacker but at the same time much land was being offered for sale—many peasants had lost everything and whole families had died off through the plague. The lords were seeking hard for tenants to settle on their demesne and did not want to buy more land with no prospects of tenants. So the craftier and richer peasants—often the village-reeves, who might also be the local money-lender—were able to take up much land at low rents. These were the employers who now competed with the nobility for men ready or able to work for wages.

And yet these rich peasants had a low social status. They belonged to a subject group, cramped by all sorts of rules and customs inside the manorial system; for that system had been worked out, not to help independent producers for the market, but to give the lord control of the peasant and to take his surplus. Unless a lord agreed to commute labour services for money, even the most purse-proud peasant could be compelled to provide a man to work three or four days a week on the demesne as well as doing extra ploughing, harrowing, mowing, reaping, carting, and so on—and to pay over, as well as a money-rent, all sorts of customary dues, like eggs at Easter and hens at Christmas.

The rich peasant, like all the villagers, had to pay the lord a yearly personal tax, tallage. He probably had to grind his corn at the lord's mill—one of the compulsions that was found most galling. When the villager brought his corn to the mill, he often had to wait valuable days for the miller's convenience and then might be cheated, while if he had a handmill at home it was liable to be destroyed on the spot if it were noticed. Further, he had

45

to bake his bread in the lord's oven, where the work was often carelessly done and he had to pay double what freemen paid for better service. He was not permitted to have an oven of his own. Again, he had to brew his ale in the lord's brewery or pay a toll in money. Often the lord had a complete monopoly; and if a serf refused his quota of ale, he still had to pay for it, and there were even times when, if he proved stubborn, the stuff was poured over his roof or doorstep.

Corn Hand-mill.

If his son sought a job outside the manor, he had to keep up a yearly payment for the right. He had to get permission and pay a fine if his son were to go to school; and he had to pay a fine, 'merchet', if he wanted to see his daughter married. He had to make a yearly payment if he brought in any wage-labour from outside the manor; he had to pay for a licence if he wanted to sell any live-stock.

Death too was a costly thing for the peasant. It might

ruin the family; for his corpse was fined by both lord and priest. The lord took his best beast as heriot, on the theory that the dead man had owed him military service and must return the armour (which in fact had never been given him); and the priest took the second best beast, on the theory that the dead man had failed to pay his full tithes when alive. As the mass of poorer peasants would not have owned more than two beasts, these

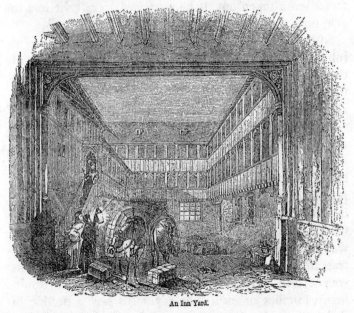

An Inn Yard.

fines meant that when the head of the family died they lost all they had. More, the heir had to pay a fine if he hoped to take over the tenement; and this entry fee was often as high as a whole year's rent or higher than it.

The tithes for the church were also a heavy burden.

A man had to pay over a tenth of his possessions, a tenth of his labour. When he cut hay, he set a tenth aside for the church; when he gathered fruit or dug roots, he set a tenth aside. Even his meagre herb-garden was taxed; he had to set aside every tenth onion or bundle of parsley. Every tenth stick he collected was not his. If his pigs dug out acorns, he must count them so that he did not rob God. Even the down of his geese must be weighed and a tenth taken out. If he exercised a craft, he had to give up a tenth of his wages.

So we need not wonder that the rich peasant was as full of grievances as the landless man. Hence the two of them often combined in the revolt. This combination gave the revolt much of its impressive size and force, but it also introduced conflicting interests.

We see then that a long fight had preceded the uprising under Wat Tyler. The peasants had become inured to daily struggle. As we saw, they even tried to use the law-courts, making the appeal to Custom that was so potent in the medieval world—though the serf could invoke action against the lord only in the latter's own Court, where he had no hope of winning. Where status was at all uncertain, the peasants struggled to be declared free; and the lord, in his need of tied labour, put all his weight into having them declared servile. As a result, many families or even whole villages saw a decline in their status. At times a village tried to prove the free status of all its people, as at Stoughton in Leicestershire (as far back as 1279) where the Abbot of Leicester was able to sway the case. In 1336 the folk of Darnell and Over in Cheshire had risen against the authority of the Cistercian monks on whose manors they dwelt.

48

Other peasants in the years nearing 1381 held up their rents, did their labour services as negligently as possible, or defaulted in the work. At times they all withdrew in a body, especially at harvest-time. They were trying to put pressure on the lords to commute their labour services and manorial dues for a fixed yearly sum of 6d. an acre. Sometimes they even made concerted attacks on the lord's officials in support of one of their group. All the while their angers were steadily gathering.

CHAPTER 4

LIFE IN THE TOWNS

EXCEPT for a few places where much trading went on, such as London and Bristol, the town populations dwindled in the fourteenth and fifteenth centuries. This decline came about through the general losses that the country experienced—as we saw above—but it was also accentuated by a movement of the highly important cloth industry to the countryside. That industry had been steadily expanding, with crucial results for the whole future of England.

If we look back at the thirteenth century, we find a certain amount of crafts practised in the villages and the manors, but entirely for local use. In the towns various articles were made for a regionally restricted market. The only article that had a wide market inside England and was even exported abroad, was cloth of a high quality; and this cloth was woven only at a few places. The craftsman in general—making cloth, metal articles, or leather wares such as shoes or saddles—was a townsman. He made and sold his goods in the same small workshop. He belonged to a craft-gild which looked after the interests of the craft, restricted output so that the market would not be glutted and prices fall, limited competition for the same reason of ensuring as prosperous a life as possible for its members, maintained prices, and had a general supervision of the supply of materials, of manufacture, and of sale of the finished articles.

Conflicts kept on breaking out, both inside a gild and between different gilds. And conflicts in the medieval world mostly ended in broken heads. Thus, joiners and saddlers were known to fight so ardently that deaths resulted, because the joiners (with whom were allied the painters and lorimers or makers of trappings for horse-bridles) complained that the saddlers wouldn't let them sell their work to anyone but the Saddlers' Company. The great gilds tried to hold down and profit from the small ones; for, in order to make one article, often several gilds had to co-operate. In particular the metal workers had a key position as they were needed by other trades to make such articles as saddles, brushes, even girdles.

Great Seal of Edward III

Members of the craft-gilds also complained that those of the merchant-gilds, who had a much better chance to amass fortunes, were getting too much power in town politics. All the while markets were expanding and by the fourteenth century the division between the crafts-men and the merchants grew sharper in the towns where trade was at all busy. One result was that the flourishing manufactures such as that of cloth wanted to get away from the towns where there was no escape from gild regulations, and to move out into the country—into Essex, Suffolk, Kent, Wiltshire, where they inevitably had strong effects on village life and began to modify the social structure, increasing the resentments that the peasants with their varying degrees of feudal bondage felt against their lords.

In the big towns a small group of leading gild-members frequently gained complete control of affairs and saw that every worth-while position was occupied by them-selves or their supporters. They showed little concern for the opinion of anyone outside their own circle, raised taxation, carried out public works, and contracted debts as they pleased. If they behaved too outrageously, the only recourse for the commoners was to start off a violent dis-pute or tumult, or attempt a law-suit which, heard before the royal Court, was likely to be ruinous. These oli-garchs or petty town-rulers were all clearly known, and when the rebels under Wat Tyler singled someone out as a 'traitor' or enemy of the people, there was nothing haphazard about it. The record of the denounced man was thoroughly known.

Attempts of journeymen to get together under the pre-tence of organizing a religious fraternity were quickly crushed; and any hasty words uttered against the dignity of a leading citizen were liable to have unfortunate con-sequences—fines or the pillory. In 1378 a parish clerk who had spoken against John of Gaunt in London was arrested by the mayor and a sheriff, and released only after abject apologies and throwing himself 'wholly on the grace of that Lord'. Six citizens had to swear to his future good behaviour on a security of £20 each.

In some towns the manorial lords had refused to make any concession and treated the whole place as their sole property. Then the townsmen were united against the lords—for instance at St. Albans and Bury St. Edmunds where the abbeys treated the places as if they were country manors and the burgesses were all serfs, and at Cambridge, where the University, then a clerical institution, sought to control the town market in its own interests. In other towns, like Canterbury and Winchester, where there were no such enemies bearing down on all the citizens, the fight between the crafts and the big merchants went on.

London was big and complicated enough to show a situation unlike any of the lesser towns. Here a deep conflict had come about between the victualling interests (fishmongers, grocers, vintners) and the drapers. The victuallers wanted to get complete control of the food market and its prices. The drapers led the smaller manufacturing groups, who wanted a free market in food. These latter also wanted to broaden the system of election to the Common Council of London so that the councillors would represent crafts rather than wards.

The drapers were allied in turn with the chief party of the nobles, that of John of Gaunt. John wanted an expedition into Spain, which was being opposed by the merchants interested in wool exports. Many London victuallers, who had tried to build up their position by dabbling in various trade enterprises, were among those thus interested. Their scheme was to attack France by way of Flanders and set up a wool-staple (a controlling trade-post) in the Netherlands. In this way the struggles among the London citizens had become linked with high politics and foreign affairs.

Servant, to prevent treachery, tasting the Wine before serving it at Table.
(Royal MS. 14 E 3.)

What further made the situation a tangled one, was the fact that the policy of cheap food was naturally popular among the poorer classes. So was the policy of broadening the elections for the Common Council. But in other respects the drapers were disliked and suspected by the commoners. Many small masters as well as the journeymen considered that the drapers kept them down and exploited them; and the weavers hated them for bringing in Flemish workers to undercut the wages of the English. On the whole the poorer craftsmen tended to support the victuallers, who at the moment were in charge of the city government, though giving way before the pressure of the drapers. The King's officials, being mostly followers of John of Gaunt, lent the drapers their support.

The resentment against the imported foreign workers was strong among the city populace, who blamed the Government for what they looked on as the unfair competition of men ready to take lower wages. For Edward III had begun the immigration by tempting over Flemings and Zealanders to Norfolk, and the Government had gone on encouraging the influx of skilled craftsmen from abroad as increasing the number of good workers available and helping to keep the pretensions of the English craftsmen down.

It was not only the poorer classes who were angered. Many of the burgesses considered the richer foreigners, sometimes a manufacturer but more often a merchant, were drawing all the wealth out of the country, especially the gold and silver, and were only bringing in useless luxuries in return. The London Merchants complained in the 1381 Parliament, 'all the gold of England, being good and heavy, was gone beyond the seas, to the great profit of those who exported it'. In 1380 a Genoese merchant, representing a syndicate of his fellow-townsmen, had tried to obtain a staple at Southampton through which Mediterranean goods would pass and which would have taken trade from London. He was murdered by some London traders.

Further, we must remember that England was in the midst of what came to be called The Hundred Years War, carrying on from 1337 to 1453. This war had mainly begun in a struggle for Gascony in south-west France, a region rich in wine, salt, iron, and ships, which imported much wheat and cloth from England. Under Edward III, who died in 1377, the nobles gave solid support to the war. There were none of the usual disorders and minor rebellions or forays which were liable to occur at home when the King and his forces were abroad. The chief reason certainly lay in the various difficulties which we have seen besetting the lords in making their manors profitable. In such a situation the lords looked to war as a useful and timely source of enrichment through loot and through selling back their prisoners for ransoms.

Such arguments and disputes as arose were mainly concerned with establishing how to finance and conduct the war, but they did not lead to any dangerous clashes. And the business of warfare, carried strenuously and steadily on, had the effect of intensifying the trend we have al-

From an Illumination, Harl. MS. 2278. Temp. Henry VI.

ready noted. Wealth and power became more and more concentrated in a few hands.

By the end of Edward III's reign, a group of less than ten great magnates had succeeded in getting hold of most of the old earldoms and baronies; and most of this group were members of royal families or closely related by blood or marriage. For the moment this concentration made for a lull in the conflicts among the nobility, which were a general condition of the feudal system despite the way in which everyone was supposed to be inter-locked in a harmonious system of loyalties and services. But the effect was soon to be very different. The situa-tion led to the long series of violent rivalries and con-flicts that marked the late fourteenth century and much of the fifteenth. For in such a closely related group of magnates it was easy for one or other to work up a claim to the throne.

Another important thing to note was the ending of the old system of knight service in return for a grant of land. This system had been an important factor in the stable working-out of feudalism, and its breakdown was one of the signs of the crisis. From Edward I, the King contracted with earls and barons to produce in the field so many fully-equipped knights and men-at-arms, on the basis of 2s. a day as payment for the ordinary knight. Now this new system was well established.

The change in military organization is reflected in the word 'soldier', which means a server-for-money, derived from the medieval Latin *solidarius*. *Solidus* meant shilling, and down to the sixteenth century there was a noun 'sold', meaning pay. At the end of the twelfth century the knight was the man taking the king's shilling—though

57

his price continued to rise. The continual warfare of the thirteenth century brought about the advent of subordinate leaders who were in effect professional soldiers. After the 1341 campaign indentured contracts between the Crown and these captains became the usual way of raising soldiers.

Monument of Edward the Black Prince, in Canterbury Cathedral.

A complicated system of contracts began to grow up. The King dealt with the great nobles, who sub-contracted to others, and so on. (Knights who commuted out of their obligations to fight took on administrative work in the counties. More and more judicial business fell into their hands, and they controlled the grand assize.)

In order to be sure of getting a good return in plunder and ransom money out of France, each noble built up a strong retinue of knights and men-at-arms, who were engaged for life on an indenture or contract. The employing noble promised a certain rate of pay, a share in plunder and ransom money, and the replacement of any horses lost in battle. In return the knight swore to serve his lord's interests in peace and war.

These retinues generally wore a livery or uniform to make clear whom they served. They became in effect small private armies, which could be highly dangerous to the Government once they were not being drawn off in foreign wars. If the barons united against the King, he was helpless. The magnates came with their armed retinues to Court or to dispense the justice that happened to please them; they stole from weaker neighbours and could not be called to account. The full effect was to come in the fifteenth century, but the system that led to so much anarchy, till curbed by the Tudors, was already in full swing.

Thus warfare was becoming more and more important for the incomes of the lords. We find the lords ranging far and wide in all sorts of wars. In a suit about the right to a certain coat-of-arms in 1386 the men deposing turned out to have been fighting in France, Spain, Greece, Egypt and various parts of the Near East as well as in eastern Europe, in Prussia, Hungary, Lithuania.

After 1360 the tide of war had turned in France. The great days of victories like Crécy, Poitiers, Sluys, and Espagnols-sur-Mer were over; and disasters such as Gaunt's expedition of 1373 arrived. From the first in Richard II's reign the ministers went on reporting to Parliament some new loss in England's lessening European empire. They had to admit that the southern coast could not be kept safe from French corsairs or the northern

Ships of the time of Richard II. (Harl. MS. 1319.)

borders from marauding Scots. 1380 saw further defeats and troubles. There was a costly and futile expedition to France, which drained the Exchequer; and the war in Flanders had brought down the export of wool into that important area. The Parliament of November was held at Northampton, to avoid the feverish and exasperated atmosphere of London.

As a result, the accord among the nobles had begun to break down before Edward III died in his dotage. An opposition had grown up, which accused the Lancastrian John of Gaunt of heading a Government that was incapable abroad and corrupt at home. The most obvious war-profiteers were Lord Latimer and the London merchants Peche and Lyons, all creatures of Gaunt. (We have met

Lyons as the adversary of Wat Tyler.) And so 1376 saw the birth of two fiercely opposing feudal parties among the nobles, whose clashes were to last, with various periods of exhaustion or truce, for over a century.

The Parliament of that year did not break Gaunt's power, but exposed the rottenness behind it, with the Speaker of the Commons as the mouthpiece of the Earl of March who led the anti-Lancastrian faction. In 1377 the boy Richard acceded to the throne.

The Government's finances were in a very bad way. And so the King's councillors turned to the poll-tax, which bore heavily on the poorer classes of the kingdom as the way out from their difficulties. The result of the efforts to enforce it was the revolt which Wat Tyler led. But the poll-tax itself, galling as it was, was only the final detail bringing to a head all the discontents which we have seen mounting in town and countryside.

CHAPTER 5

JOHN BALL

DISCONTENTS, however wide and strong, do not lead to a revolt like that of 1381, with its definite and consistent programme of reform, unless men have done a lot of hard thinking and unless there are leaders who can crystallize the main lines of thought, providing slogans and easily-grasped goals.

First, we must note that the medieval peasants and craftsmen had their own traditions, expressed in songs, tales, proverbs, and customary lore, and also in games and rites, above all the rites of May Day. In the songs they expressed their anger against oppression and cele-brated the heroes, real or imaginary, who had fought the oppressors—Hereward the Wake and Robin Hood and many others. In the games and rites they crowned their own kings of jollity and happiness; and even jested at the existing state of things by setting up mock kings for the time of a festival, Harvest-Lords, Abbots of Bon Accord, and Twelfth Night Kings—any title that ex-pressed a reversal of the roles that ruled in everyday life.

They had their tradition of what we may call primi-tive democracy, put in neat form in the couplet that played its part in provoking the 1381 revolt:

When Adam delved and Eve span,
Who was then the Gentleman?

The efforts made to invoke 'Domesday Book', which we have noted, seem to have had behind them a conviction that in the days before the Normans the peasantry had not yet fallen into bondage. And a strong impulse to such attitudes had long been given by the preaching of the friars, who practised evangelic poverty and wandered about among the people. The poet Langland, writing a few years before the rebellion in the old Anglo-Saxon alliterative style, without rhymes, tells us of the preachers:

They preach to men of poverty and prove it by Seneca that all things under heaven ought to be in common.

Most of the friars no doubt did not mean their doctrines of the holiness of poverty and their denunciations of wealth to be given a political interpretation. But naturally the peasants were liable to feel that what was said had a high relevance to their own troubles, grievances, and hopes, and that the preachings went far to justify their desire to take action.

Occasionally indeed a friar was himself moved to urge the people to resist the lords. We hear of a Franciscan friar who stirred up the tenants of the monastery of Middleton to combine against the abbot; and after the revolt there were many accusations that the friars had been to blame for the way the people had risen, to which they indignantly replied.

However, the man who took the doctrine of holy

poverty to heart and transformed it into a revolutionary creed was John Ball, the priest who was lying in the dungeons of Maidstone jail, waiting for the rebellion that he had done so much to bring about.

Friar Preaching from a Moveable Pulpit—(Royal MS. 14 E. iii).

Soon after the Black Death he had come to Colchester from St. Mary's in York, where he had been a secular priest. For some thirty years he made Colchester his centre. He seems to have been a parochial chaplain—a kind of priest that had much the same level in the Church as a craftsman had among the laity. The chaplains had charge of the churches, and the large number of the higher parish clergy killed off by the plague gave them an increased importance. They were the priests who, close to the people, were rebuked by the Archbishop for asking for better wages. Many of them sided with the people during the rebellion, unlike the higher clergy or the monks.

Tradition suggests that Ball was chaplain of St. James at Colchester for a while. And when he was denounced by the Archbishop and lost his position, he continued to work from Colchester, wandering about the country-side and tirelessly preaching against the rich men and the lords. He attacked tithes and serfdom, and told the peasants that it was to be their work to bring about a different and a better world.

Informations were laid against him. At some date between 1362 and 1366 he was excommunicated by Simon Islip, Archbishop of Canterbury. Islip wanted to stop the growing host of irregular preachers and he naturally dealt with Ball. He accused him of unfairly claiming the dignity of priest and of preaching manifold errors and scandals, tending to the loss of his own soul and the damnation of his listeners as well as to the open shame of the Church. He commanded everyone to withdraw under pain of excommunication from his sermons and to avoid them in future, and Ball himself to be examined on matters 'touching the correction and salvation of his soul'.

The next archbishop, Simon Langham, in 1366 bade the rural dean of Bocking in Essex to threaten with excommunication all who hearkened to Ball, and to order Ball to appear before him, Langham, for correction.

Ball took no notice, but went on with his preaching and exhortation. Then in the second year of Simon Sudbury's accession as Archbishop, in December 1376, the King, at Sudbury's complaint, issued letters patent to five commissioners from Colchester and its district, who were to arrest Ball as a contumacious and excommunicated fellow. But they do not seem to have been able to lay hands on him. On the eve of the revolt he was still at liberty.

The ease with which Ball remained freely roaming about and fierily preaching to the peasants suggests that he was much loved and that whenever an attempt was made to find him he was able to find secure shelter. Over some twenty years he seems to have been caught only three times. Without an almost unanimous support among the countryfolk he could never have carried on so long.

Archbishop reading a Papal Bull. (Harl. MS. 1319.)

On 26 April 1381 Sudbury sent out a writ to the officials and clergy of the diocese of Canterbury, which showed how infuriated he felt. The writ recounted how Ball, in spite of the earlier decrees of excommunication, had scorned to seek absolution, but had 'slunk back to our diocese, like the fox that evaded the hunter, and feared not to preach and argue both in the churches and church-yards (without the leave or against the will of the paro-chial authorities) and also in markets and other profane places, there beguiling the ears of the laity by his invec-tives and putting about such scandals concerning our per-son and those of other prelates and clergy and—what is worse—using concerning the Holy Father himself language such as shamed the ears of good Christians'.

This statement brings out the fearless and open way in which Ball had so long gone about with his defiant speeches. However, its stern call for action drove the authorities to make a special effort. Ball was at last arrested and put into Maidstone jail, where soon after the rebels broke in and rescued him, as he prophesied to his jailers.

What did Ball preach to the peasants which they found so much to their liking? *The Chronicle of England* tells us plainly that he declared, 'At the beginning all were created equal. It is the tyranny of perverse men which has caused servitude to arise, in spite of God's law; if God had willed that there should be serfs, He would have said at the beginning of the world who should be serf and who should be lord.'

Froissart, the French chronicler, who spent several years in England and did not die till 1410, gives us a longer version. He says that there was 'a crazy priest in the county of Kent, called John Ball, who for his absurd preaching had been three times confined to prison'. Ball was accustomed to gather a crowd round him in the market-place and then preach to them:

'My good friends, matters cannot go well in England until all things be held in common; when there shall be neither vassals nor lords; when the lords shall be no more masters than ourselves. How ill they behave to us! For what reason do they hold us in bondage? Are we not all descended from the same parents, Adam and Eve? And what can they show, or what reason can they give, why they should be more masters than ourselves? They are clothed in velvet and rich stuffs, ornamented with ermine and other furs, while we are forced to wear poor clothing. They have wine, spices, and fine bread, while we have only rye, and the refuse of the straw; and when we drink, it must be water. They have handsome seats

Female Costume, time of Richard II
(Royal MS. 16 G. v., and Harleian MS. 4379.)

and manors, while we must brave the wind and rain in our labours in the field; and it is by our labours that they have wherewith to support their pomp. We are called slaves, and if we do not perform our service we are beaten, and we have no sovereign to whom we can complain or who would be willing to hear us. Let us go to the King and remonstrate with him, he is young and from him we may obtain a favourable answer, and if not, we must ourselves seek to amend our conditions.'

And, Froissart adds, the people 'would murmur one with another in the fields and in the ways as they went together how John Ball said truth'.

The higher clergy must have been much annoyed by his insistence that no tithes should be given to them, 'except the party that shall give the same were richer than the vicar or parson that shall receive it'.

We do not know what he looked like. But the poet William Morris in Victorian days, in his tale *A Dream of John Ball*, imagines him preaching on a village green, 'clad in a long brown gown of coarse wool, girt with a cord, to which hung a pair of beads—or rosary as we should call it today—and a book in a bag. The man was tall and bigboned, a ring of dark hair surrounded his priest's tonsure; his nose was big but clear cut with wide nostrils; his shaven face showed a longish upper lip and a big but blunt chin; his mouth was big and the lips closed firmly; a face not very noteworthy but for his grey eyes well-opened and wide apart, at whiles lighting up his whole face with a kindly smile, at whiles set and stern; at whiles resting in that look as if they were gazing at something a long way off; which is the wont of the poet or enthusiast . . . And the man stood still for a while eyeing the throng. Sometimes he caught the eye of one or another and then that kindly smile spread over his face, but faded off into the sternness and sadness of a man who has heavy and great thoughts about him.'

And Morris imagines himself among the listeners— 'a great expectation had fallen by now on all that throng,

69

and no word was spoken even in a whisper, and all men's hearts and eyes were fixed upon the dark figure standing straight up now by the tall white shaft of the cross, his hands stretched out before him, one palm laid upon the other. And as for me, as I made ready to hearken, I felt a joy in my soul that I had never yet felt.'

Several of his letters or messages have luckily come down to us. Doubtless some had been sent out from Maidstone jail as he felt sure that the hour of action was nearing. But as they are written in a sort of code, he must have been in the habit of using this method of communication among those whom he knew well and trusted; otherwise he could not have been confident that their meaning would have been clearly understood. They thus give us a fascinating glimpse of the way the revolt had been prepared for by men like Ball and Tyler, the way they thought, and the sort of language that the medieval peasant used when he was talking to his fellows and wanted to hide his purposes from the lords and their followers.

First here is a quatrain where the bell-ringing is a simple emblem for the moment of gathering together in revolt:

John Ball greeteth you all
And doth to understand he hath rung your bell.
Now with right and might, wit and skill,
God speed every dell.

(He lets them understand or know that he has rung their bell; and God is called on to speed the whole venture.)

Another message which holds his name is this:

John Ball, St. Mary priest, greeteth well all manner of men and biddeth them in the name of the Trinity, Father, Son and Holy Ghost, stand manlike together in truth, and help truth, and truth shall help you:

> Now reigneth price in price,
> Covetise is holden wise,   (*Greed*)
> Lechery without shame,
> Gluttony without blame,
> Envy reigneth with reason,
> And Sloth is taken in great season.
> God do bote for now is time.

('God exact the penalty', is the message of the last line.)

Another message mentions Ball under the name of John Sheep. This seems to have been an earlier letter passed round in which he bids men prepare for action; at the time of its writing he was in Colchester.

John Sheep, sometime St. Mary priest of York, and now in Colchester, greeteth well John Nameless and John Miller and John Carter, and biddeth them that they beware of guile in borough and standeth together in God's name and biddeth Piers Plowman to go to his work and chastise well Hob the Robber, and take with him John Trueman and all his fellows and no more, and look that you shape to one head and no more.

Ball is giving good counsel as well as encouragement. The three Johns, Nameless, Miller, and Carter, were probably real persons disguised by pseudonyms similar to Ball's own

71

one of John Sheep. Ball bids them take care whom they
trust: there is guile in borough—probably the richer
townsmen are liable to lay information if they suspect
trouble. Ball calls for unity among the men devoted to
the cause (John Trueman and all his fellows), and uses
the same name Piers Plowman to represent the peasantry
as did the poet Langland in his great poem that had
been composed in the years leading up to the revolt. Ball
ends by advising the rebels to choose a single leader and
to be faithful to him—advice that they thoroughly carried out in electing Wat Tyler and remaining whole-
hearted in their acceptance of his lead. Hob the Robber
is Sir Robert Hales, the King's treasurer. In naming him
as the enemy of the people, Ball is denouncing all the
persons who had taken an active part in carrying out the
Government's policy.

Horse beating a Tabor.

There are some other messages which are worth quot-
ing as they help to bring strongly before us the atmosphere of the times, and the heady excitement of the con-
spiratorial work that must have gone on in the weeks
leading up to June 1381.

Jack Carter prays you all that you make a good end of that you have begun, and doth well, and aye better and better, for at the evening men heareth the day. For if the end be well, then all is well.

Let Piers the Plowman my brother dwell at home and dight (prepare) us corn, and I will go with you and help that I may dight you meat and drink, that you none fail. Look that Hob Robber be well chastised for laying of your grace, for you have great need to take God with you in all your deeds. For now is time to be ware.

Here again we meet Jack Carter, Piers Plowman, and Hob the Robber. The call to do well and to do better is of much interest; for it again suggests a link with Langland's poem, where Piers Plowman sets out in search of Do Well and Do Better. Do Well is the protector and friend of men who live by honest labour and do not injure their neighbours, while Do Better helps those in need and preaches to the poor.

Another message runs in rough verse:

John Miller asketh help to turn his mill right:
He hath ground small, small,
The King's Son of Heaven will pay for it all,
Look the mill go right, with its four sails dight,
With right and with might, with skill and with will,
And let the post stand in steadfastness,
Let right help might, and skill go before will,
Then shall our mill go aright.
But if might go before right, and will go before skill,
Then is our mill mis-a-dight.

Beware ere you be woe.
Know your friend from your foe,
Take enough and cry Ho!
And do well and better and flee sin,
And seek our peace and dwell therein,
So biddeth John Trueman and all his friends.

Again we meet Do Well and Do Better. Ball uses the image of the mill to express the movements of society. (The 'post' is the central mill-post.) He says that if right controls might or power, and if skill (knowledge and the practical lore of labour) controls will or mere desire and power, then all will be well. Again he warns his followers to distinguish with care between friend and foe.

Finally we have a message from Jack Trueman:

Jack Trueman doth you to understand
That falsehood and guile hath reigned too long
And truth hath been set under a lock
And falseness reigneth in every flock,
No man may come truth to   (*may come to truth*)
But he must sing *si dedero*.   (*if I will give*)
Speak, spend and speed, quoth John of Bathon

(*a bishop*)

And therefore sin fareth as wild flood,
True love is away that was so good
God do bote, for now is time.   (*God, give redress*)

It is tempting to think that John or Jack Trueman, as well as standing for the faithful supporters of the revolt in general, was a particular pseudonym standing for Wat Tyler, and that Wat had been working with John Ball in the earlier messages which had been sent out.

But now the rebellion itself is calling us. However, before we turn to the stirring events, it is worth while noting again how close we feel in Langland's poem to the world revealed by the darkly-worded messages of John Ball. Langland begins with a vision of a great gathering of people:

I had wondered me weary, so weary I rested me
On a broad bank by a merry-sounding burn;
And as I lay and leaned and looked into the waters
I slumbered in a sleeping, it rippled so merrily.
And I dreamed, marvellously.
All the world's weal, all the world's woe,
Truth and trickery, treason and guile,
All I saw, sleeping.
I was in a wilderness, wist I not where,
And eastward I looked against the sun.
I saw a Tower on an hill, fairly fashioned,
Beneath it a Dell, and in the Dell a dungeon,
With deep ditches and dark, dreadful to see,
And Death and wicked spirits dwelt therein,
And all between, between the Hill and Dungeon,
A fair Field full of Folk.
Rich and poor, all manner of men,
Working and wandering, as in the world we must.
Some were for ploughing and played full seldom,
Set their seed and sowed their seed, and sweated hard,
To win what wastrels with gluttony destroyed.

Langland is thinking of earthly life, set between heaven and hell, but the picture he draws is also that of the peasants desperately toiling, with the threatening Tower of the manor-lord set above them and the Dungeons of his displeasure ready to take them if they resisted. And though he is thinking only in moral terms in his call for men to unite in living a good life, he makes us think of Ball fervently asking them to unite steadfastly in the effort to Do Well and Do Better, despite the threats of might and will.

'I counsel you,' says Conscience, 'come with me, you fools,
Into the Fort of Unity, and hold we us there,
Cry we to Nature to come and defend us
From the hurts of the fiend for love of Piers Plowman.
Cry we to all the Commons to come into Unity
And there to abide and fight against Belial's children.'

76

CHAPTER 6

THE REVOLT IN
FULL SWING

On 7 June the rebels of Kent elected Wat Tyler as their leader, and this decision was accepted whole-heartedly also in Essex and East Anglia. On the 8th and 9th, with Maidstone still as the centre, the revolt swept through Kent. The speed of the response here as elsewhere showed how men were waiting impatiently for the signal. The large numbers of official rolls in the houses of Thomas Shardelow of Dartford, coroner of Kent, and of Elias Raynor of Strood were all burned in the streets. The big manor house of Nicholas Herring of North Cray was broken into, and the goods and cattle were sold cheaply to the peasants of the neighbourhood—the proceeds being used for the army funds. Recruits flocked in from all the villages between the Weald and the Thames estuary.

Four leading members of the gentry were taken and kept as prisoners after they had sworn the oath of allegiance to King Richard and the True Commons. In no case did the peasant rebels wantonly massacre. During their period of triumph they executed a number of men, but these were invariably known for their misdeeds and opressions, and strongly identified with the system against which the peasants were protesting. Anger was directed primarily against royal officials, lawyers, followers of John of Gaunt, and particularly harsh landlords.

Tyler, as soon as he became leader, issued a proclamation in which he stated that the people in arms continued allegiance to Richard and the Commons, but would accept no king named John—that is, would not accept the continued domination of John of Gaunt. They would not agree to any further tax being levied in the kingdom and held that the only necessary tax was that of Fifteenth. Tyler added that they would be ready to support their cause whenever called on. Clearly he and the people believed that if only they could separate the young king, now about fourteen years old, from the councillors, they could draw him into championing their rights.

On the 10th a further important move was made. At the head of the main body of his host, Tyler proceeded to Canterbury, the chief town in Kent, with its ancient archbishopric, its pilgrim-thronged and bejewelled tomb of St. Thomas Becket. The men marched in good order, halting all travellers, especially the pilgrims, to teach them the aims of the uprising and the new oath of allegiance. (As the pilgrims would be returning home all over England, they would serve as excellent carriers of news about the rising and would be able to give their towns and villages precise information.)

St. Thomas Becket, because he had been martyred for defying a king, was deeply reverenced and loved by the commoners. In 1370, the year of the jubilee pilgrimage, Simon Sudbury, then Bishop of London, had come upon a band of pilgrims pressing along the London road to Canterbury, and he had denounced them for hoping to get special indulgences or pardons on such a year. Sudbury, an intelligent man, was meaning to rebuke the pilgrims for superstitious beliefs, but they took his words as an insult to the great saint-martyr. Some of them were too aghast to speak, others yelled curses on the Bishop. One Kentishman, Thomas of Aldon, rode furiously up to him and cried out, 'My Lord Bishop, for this act of yours, stirring the people to sedition against St. Thomas, I stake the satisfaction of my soul that you will close your life by a most terrible death.' And the crowd of pilgrims answered with a shout of Amen.

Drummers. (Engraved by Strutt, from the Liber Regalis, Westminster Abbey.)

This tale must have been told and retold as the host marched on along the dusty roads. June was not one of the busiest months of the year for a peasant, but it had its many tasks. The threshing floor must be got ready, cleaned of straw, dirt, and dust; meadows might be cut, barley be mown, and corn be threshed for sowing. Also, any manure available might be carried to the fields, fuel collected, early fat sheep shorn, tender herbs sown, plants and herbs distilled. But not many of these tasks were urgent, and the peasants could look happily out on the fields as they passed, without feeling that their own places would be suffering neglect.

Near noon they entered the town. No opposition was made and cheering citizens lined the cobbled streets. During the midday High Mass a large detachment of the rebels pushed their way into the cathedral and 'made a reverence and cried with one voice to the monks to choose a monk for Archbishop of Canterbury'. Tyler stated from the pulpit that Sudbury had been condemned as a traitor and would be duly executed when caught. The rebels shouted that they would root him out in London and free the King from his hands. Despite episodes like Sudbury's rebuke of the pilgrims, the people hated him for

Convocation of Clergy. (From the Harl. MS. 4379.)

his political role as chancellor, not for his position in the Church.

Clerics played an essential part in the machinery of government. They did much in running the local as well as the central organs of control. Many of the administrative officials were clerics: for instance, the Receiver-General and the lesser receivers of Gaunt's Duchy of Lancaster. The sheriff of each county town could not get along without a staff of clerks; and officials such as coroners, escheators, bailiffs, and so on, were in the same position. As much local government (in areas called liberties or franchises) was still in private hands, under barons, abbots, bishops, the clerics carried on at all levels of the administration there; and things were the same in the church's vast estates. Indeed, practically all records and accounts were kept by clerics; and records, as we have seen, were abhorred by the people for being used against them to prove their enslaved status.

After stating the rebels' decision about Sudbury, Tyler left the cathedral and rode back to the town centre. There, before the large assembly of the citizens and the insurgent forces, the Mayor and Bailiff, as well as other leading citizens, swore the new oath of loyalty and accepted Tyler's programme. Canterbury thus became the first town where the officials together with the citizens acclaimed the new rule and swore to administer things according to its principles.

Meanwhile, other rebels sacked the castle and broke open the prison. They brought the fettered and manacled men and women out of the dungeons. Others again carefully searched the palace for all rolls and records, which were piled up and burned. The peasants and craftsmen

81

wandered through the rich tapestried halls and chambers, looking for any sign of Sudbury. One of them remarked. 'The Chancellor of England has had this piece of furniture very cheap. Now he must give us an account of his revenue and of the very large sums which he has levied since the coronation of the King.' The county Sheriff was captured and made to hand over his store of papers, which were burned in the street. But though one of the most hated officials, he was not killed.

Then, however, the rebels asked the citizens, 'Have you not some traitors here?' Three men were pointed out. They were promptly dragged through the streets and beheaded. The houses of others were broken into and sacked. More and more documents, leases, bonds, and the like were destroyed. Even after Tyler withdrew with his troops, for several days the folk of Canterbury went on breaking into the houses of men whom they had marked down as their oppressors.

After the various ceremonies, Tyler accepted 500 new recruits, then bade the other citizens stay at home and order the town according to the new system. Here, as throughout his career of command, we see Tyler acting with a carefully thought-out plan of procedure. His announcement that Sudbury was condemned, we may take as coming from a decision reached by the rebel council at Maidstone. By making it dramatically public from the Archbishop's own pulpit, he added to its effect of authority and prepared men's minds for what was to come later in London. The election of a new archbishop was one of the main demands of the rebels. They had definite and drastic views on the need to reform the Church; and as the archbishopric was one of the very highest offices in the realm, usually leading to great secular powers as well as ecclesiastical, they must have discussed what reliable man they could choose to fill it. There can be no doubt that they had decided to see John Ball the next Archbishop of Canterbury, to match Wat Tyler as the Chancellor.

Tyler marched his forces back to Maidstone, where he was received with the same enthusiasm as at Canterbury. The chief jailer of the castle, with some other nobles, was arrested and carried off as a hostage, with the army. The families of the hostages were not molested, though attacks were made on some of the administrators, such as Thomas Hazelden. His manors were treated like those of Herring at North Cray; the corn and the stock were sold cheaply to the peasants.

Among Tyler's lieutenants we hear of John Hales of Malling, Alan Threder, William Hawke, John Ferrour, as well as Jack Straw, a strange figure who flits across both the Kentish and the Essex scene. Later, chroniclers and balladists confused him with Wat himself, but the Rolls of Parliament and a contemporary history carefully distinguish the two men. 'Jack Straw' may have been a real name, though it sounds rather like one of the assumed names of plotters in John Ball's messages. (A Jack Rackstraw is also mentioned later in some of the legal proceedings; he made a proclamation to the people of the Island of Thanet. He seems the same person.) Jack may have been one of the small band of men, mainly of Essex, who seem to have been in touch with John Ball for some time, and who may be called the underground organizers of the rebellion. Not that we should overstress what they did. It is unlikely that there was any elaborate organization.

The emotions of revolt had long been simmering; and it needed little to convert the local groups of peasants, who had sometimes had experience as defiant conventicles, into a united army of rebels. Still, the existence of a tough though small body of devoted rebels, who were able at once to come forward as leaders and to build up an effective co-ordination between the districts, may well have helped to give the uprising its remarkably rapid and powerful thrust. In any event, John Ball's long work of preaching a rebellious brotherhood must have developed many men of a bold and determined nature to the point of impatiently waiting for the first chance of coming forward as leaders. Jack Straw, like Wat Tyler, seems certainly one of these fiery characters who had been biding their time.

We also know of at least one member of the gentry in Kent, a squire named Bertram Wilmington, who raised a band at Wye in the name of the people; and among the supporters were a sprinkling of rich yeomen and priests—for instance, John Covershurst of Lamberhurst, who held a freehold farm of over 120 acres and who was later executed by the Government. But most of the marchers were craftsmen and peasants, smallholders or labourers.

On 11 and 12 June the rebel army proceeded with good speed to the outskirts of London. All the while more recruits flocked in. Froissart tells us, 'They set out at early morning, and all the folk of Canterbury with them, and took the road to Rochester. And they carried with them all the village folk from the right hand and from the left; and they went on their way like a tempest, sweeping and casting down all houses of lawyers and proctors of the King's or Archbishop's Courts, on whom they had no mercy.'

Lawyers were mostly laymen. They were in the thick of the political issues, and presided over the public or private Courts through which the Government was carried on, or pleaded before them. Their work brought them into close contact with all the great of the land, the King and the members of his administration, the chief lords, whether secular or ecclesiastical. As the power of the

Law Habits of the fifteenth century. (Collected from various contemporary MSS. Engraved in Strutt's 'Angel-Cynnan.')

lords was based in controlling the land and in drawing rents and services from the peasants, the lawyers were experts in all legal matters connected with landed estates. They it was who had worked out the legal details of the developed system tying the peasant to the soil, and who at assize time appeared in the shires as judges and officials to prove the lord in the right whatever he did— though they were also experts in the laws and customs which laid down the relations of the King and his barons. But whatever varying part they might play in the wider political field, they were agreed in the right of the lord to hold his peasants in servitude, and were never keener than when defending and expounding this right of his. No wonder then that the commoners saw them as a sort of devils who plagued them and blocked all the roads to freedom that seemed to open up.

Many were the songs and satirical poems of the period that told how justice was sold for money and that the poor had no hope with the lawyers; and we may be sure that some of these songs mingled with chants about Robin Hood and other bold outlaws as the rebels marched on to the great city of London. A few years later a poet, perhaps John Lydgate, was to tell how the man without money in his purse could have no success in the law courts.

> To London once my steps I bent,
> Where truth in no wise should be faint;
> To Westminster-ward I forthwith went,
> To a man of law to make complaint;
> I said, 'For Mary's sake, that holy saint,
> Pity the poor that would proceed.'
> But for lack of money I could not speed.
>
> And as I thrust the press among,
> By froward chance my hood was gone;
> Yet for all that I stayed not long,
> Till to the King's Bench I was come.
> Before the judge I kneeled anon,
> And prayed him for God's sake to take heed;
> But for lack of money I might not speed.

Beneath him sat clerks a great crowd,
Who fast did write with one assent.
There stood up one and cried aloud,
'Richard, Robert, and John of Kent.'
I knew not well what this man meant,
He cried so rapidly there indeed.
But he that lacked money might not speed.

Lydgate presenting his Poem of 'The Pilgrim,' to the Earl of
Warwick and Salisbury. (Harleian, MS. No. 4826.)

Songs in this vein would have sounded through the June
sunlight, punctuated by jovial bursts of laughter, as the
peasant army marched on London, led by Wat Tyler and
John Ball.

As they neared the city, they met the King's mother, Joan of Kent, widow of the Black Prince, who had been with a retinue on a pilgrimage to the Kentish shrines. She was now hurrying back to get behind the strong walls of the Tower. The fact that she had left her return so late shows how the Government had failed to realize the gravity of the situation and then had waited in a state of paralysis. When she and her attendants came up against the host of roughly-armed peasants, they gave themselves up for lost; but to their surprise they suffered nothing worse than a brief arrest. After making a few jests, the leaders of the band that had stopped her gave orders for the party to be allowed to proceed, unmolested and unplundered.

In Essex too, things had been moving. Colchester's capture had involved the slaughter of several Flemings, and a Fleming was killed also at Manningtree. The killing of Flemings, which was the one blot on the rebellion, must have been the work, not of peasants, but of disgruntled town craftsmen.

Religious houses were attacked as well as manors but the motive was the same in both cases. Thus, at the great Abbey of Waltham, many documents were burned. Inevitably, some individuals tried to take advantage of the general disorder to further their own claims. We hear of men who had claims of contested value to various manors or lands and who called in the rebels. The latter, ready to champion any protests against the lords in possession, installed the new claimants, no doubt getting from them an assurance that old servitudes would be wiped out.

On 11 June the Essex host set out to march on London.

Clearly, there was close and effective liaison with Wat Tyler. Among the Essex leaders were Thomas Farringdon, a Londoner, Henry Baber of Manningtree, Adam Mitchell, and John Starling. According to later reports, Farringdon was the chief, and we may assume that he had Essex connexions of some kind.

By the evening of Wednesday the 12th, the men of Kent were encamped on Blackheath, and those of Essex in the fields by Mile End, outside the north-east corner of the city walls. At least 30,000 rebels had marched in from the south, and perhaps about the same number from Essex—while inside London, with its population of 40,000 to 50,000 citizens, at least half—'small folk', says Froissart—were eager to hail the True Commons. All the while more recruits were coming in.

As Wat led his men in to their encampments, a messenger came from the King, asking what was the intention of the host. Wat replied by protesting loyalty and zeal for the honour of England; the people wanted only to lay before the King their complaints and grievances against his uncles and ministers who had so misgoverned the realm. The bearer of the rebels' reply was the constable of Rochester Castle who was being held as a hostage. To ensure his return, Tyler still held his two sons.

Meanwhile, the more ardent of Tyler's force pushed on as far as Southwark and Lambeth, where they were met by large numbers of sympathizers from the suburbs and from the city itself, who had come across the Thames in small ferries. The drawbridge in the middle of London Bridge had been raised at the news of the rebels' approach, and the bridge could not be crossed.

A detachment was sent to break open the two South-wark prisons, the Marshalsea, and the King's Bench. They freed the prisoners and fired the buildings. These jails were specially hated, as men convicted of infringing the Statute of Labourers were sent to them. A lawsuit of 1382 gives us a chance glimpse of the street scene at this moment. A goldsmith, John de Salesbury, was suing a chaplain, William de Denton, about the ownership of three buildings with outhouses in Southwark. When the case came up again after the revolt, William pleaded that the writ should be quashed, as John, while the action was pending, had entered the premises. John replied, 'In the detestable tumult, which recently arose, many male-factors, overthrowers of society, pulled down and destroyed a messuage next to the said tenements, whereupon I, fearing that the malefactors would pull down and destroy the said tenements, went on my knees before them in the street, telling them that the said tenements had been at one time my ancestors' and that I had a certain writ pending concerning these tenements in the King's Court against William, begging and praying them especially for the love of God not to do any damage to the said tenements, and I did not enter the tenements.'

The rebel vanguard next marched on two more miles and sacked the Archbishop's Palace at Lambeth. They also burned down the house of the Marshalsea Warden. The flames leaped up all night and Londoners crowded the wharves or peered from their upper windows to watch. The glow invaded the rooms of the King and his councillors in the Tower.

The whole city was in a ferment. Apprentices, journey-men, and even some of the masters were getting ready to join the rebels. Previously the mob of apprentices had been high-spiritedly ready to fight for whichever group of masters paid best; but the discontents which had long been growing in their ranks made them feel in complete accord with the attackers. They planned to force the city gates from within and admit the rebels without waiting for an assault on the walls.

Water Tournament.

The gates and walls were the defences of London, and the royalists in the city Government, led by the Lord Mayor, William Walworth, had done their best to guard them. English cities in general were less well-defended than cities on the Continent; but London had a wall, twenty feet high, with battlements outside and a broad ledge inside for the defenders to stand on. Below, outside, there ran a ditch, which at its largest, near the Tower, was some 100 feet wide. West of the Tower it curved northward, followed the walls round, and joined the Fleet River (flowing where now is Farringdon Street). The weakest section of the defences lay on the Thames side; for an enemy who controlled the river could easily land there.

Cannon already existed. At least three small guns seem used at Crécy in 1346, though the battle was decided by the English longbow; and by 1360 the Tower of London had four guns. After 1380 the accounts for saltpetre, sulphur, and guns grew numerous. Tyler's revolt thus occurred just as cannon were coming in; but there is no indication that guns played any part in the fighting on either side. Cannon were still incompetent and liable to blow up, as they continued to be till they were moulded of one piece of metal. To break through walls, pioneers had usually to mine under them, then prop them up with timber, which was set on fire. As the wood charred, the walls collapsed and the attackers charged through the breach. But unless they were in very strong force or had support from within, they were liable to be trapped in the narrow entry. (Later, in 1471, a band of Lancastrians burned down thirteen houses on the Bridge and ferried 5,000 men from Surrey to fight their way through Aldgate; but once they were inside the gate, the portcullis was lowered and they were cut down in the narrow streets.)

The walls were probably not in a good condition. Medieval men had little respect for public works. They often wrecked the highways by digging clay out of them; in 1310 they stole stones from the London walls and 'timber from the gates and postern aforesaid in contempt of themselves, and to the detriment of our city aforesaid, and the manifest peril of all dwelling within', as an ordinance declared. A tax called 'murrage' was levied for repairing the walls; but it was farmed out like many other taxes, and not much of it ever reached the public purse. A number of persons, from the King and Queen down to the mayor and aldermen, took part of the money as gifts to themselves. Five years after Tyler's revolt, when there was the scare of a French invasion, an extensive murrage-tax was granted, covering a vast amount of articles, from wax, almonds, rice, to cloth, corn, fish. It suggests that the defences had been let decay rather badly.

The gates were the key-points. Even in the most quiet times of peace, they were guarded. When night fell, the curfew was first tolled by St. Martin's-le-Grand (a thief's sanctuary, where now rises the G.P.O.), and then all the parish churches echoed the toll. The order ran that 'all the Gates are to be shut, as well as all taverns for wine or for ale; and no one is to go about the streets or ways. Six persons are to watch in each Ward by night, of the most competent men of the Ward thereto; and the two serjeants who guard the Gates by day, are to lie at night either within the Gates, or near thereto.' The watch patrolled the streets, calling the hours and arresting anyone found abroad in the streets. They took the arrested person to a small prison in Cornhill, the Tun, where he or she was detained for trial in the morning.

At the approach of any danger, the citizens were called to arms and could be relied on to man the gates and walls. But in a case like the 1381 revolt, when so many of them were partisans of the attackers, the call was not of much use and indeed was likely to produce dangers for the authorities.

Walworth, the Lord Mayor, a speculator who belonged to the victualling party and who drew much of his income from haunts of vice, acted as vigorously as was possible in the situation. He had the gates closed and the

93

drawbridge raised; and he took care that the ward-aldermen in charge of the key-posts belonged to his own party. But three of these men—Walter Sybyle, William Tonge, and John Horne—had close links with the rebels; and they somehow managed to be put over the wards connected with the main city gates: the Bridge Ward, where the fishmongers were in strength, and the Aldgate, where the butchers and poulterers gathered. As a result, the rebels had friends ready to let them in if they were denied entry.

London Bridge, Southwark side.

Walworth sent out a deputation of citizens, composed of Horne, Adam Carlyll, and John Fresh, to warn the rebel host not to approach London, which, he declared, would be strongly defended. Horne, however, succeeded in getting a word aside with Wat. He told him to disregard the threat and to advance with all speed, as preparations for admitting him were completed and the

94

people of London supported the revolt. When the rebels marched in, said Horne, 'They'd be lovingly received in the city, as a father by his children, or as a friend by his friend'.

Horne indeed stayed with the rebels till night came down. Then he smuggled three of them into the city and gave them shelter in his house. Some of their chief London adherents came there for a discussion and the final plans for the taking of London were made. While this conference was going on. Horne rode off to Walworth. He told him that he had spoken with the rebels, conveyed the warning, and found them still resolved to march on London. However, he went on, there was no need for the Lord Mayor to be afraid for his city; he swore by his head that the rebels were honest folk who would not do a pennyworth of damage.

All the while the revolt was spreading. The speedy organizing power shown by the peasants was remarkable. Essex leaders had been sending out messages since 1 June, and the word for revolt had gone across all East Anglia. Other messengers were at work in Surrey and in Sussex. The Suffolk leaders were already at Blackheath, in council with Wat Tyler and John Ball and the other leaders of the host. The men of Hertford sent representatives to the army of Essex at Mile End. All the afternoon and evening messengers were riding out from the camps, on the roads stretching north, south, east, and west, while groups came in from the near counties to discuss arrangements with Wat Tyler or his lieutenants. Other delegates were on their way, riding fast, from the more outlying shires of the west and the Midlands.

CHAPTER 7

FIRST PARLEYS

WHAT were the Court and its notables doing all this time? They were doing nothing. This will seem surprising until we realize that the King had no standing army and no police force. He depended for any large armed body on his nobles. Each lord had his personal group of retainers; but unless the King had time to call out his lords and the lords had time to call out their forces and muster them, he was more or less powerless against any unexpected attack in mass. At any time, if the barons did not respond to his call, he was lost, as was to happen to Richard II himself in 1399 when Bolingbroke raised the banner of dynastic revolt and made himself Henry IV.

Further, as was shown clearly by the actions taken to deal with the riots at Brentwood which precipitated the national rebellion, the King's councillors had no notion at all of the temper of the country or the fact that the people had been driven to the edge of desperation. The great lords had such a contempt for commoners, especially for the peasantry, that they could not consider them a serious threat. For them it was so absolutely against the nature of things for such curs and swine to stand up against their masters, they could scarcely conceive it even

Richard II. and Bolingbroke arrived at London.

when it happened before their own eyes and even though
they had witnessed a violent peasants' revolt, the Jacquerie, a few years earlier in France.

The lords' view of the peasants can be seen in the
grotesque descriptions we find in the literature composed for them. In French feudal verse—the epical tales
or *chansons de geste*—we read:

> The villeins are uglily designed,
> The ugliest things a man could find;
> Each of them is fifteen feet,
> You'd think it's giants that you meet,
> But there's no ugliness they lack,
> Humped in front, humped at the back.

And this is how a typical peasant is described in the romance of *Aucassin and Nicolette*: 'Tall he was, and marvellously ugly and hideous. His head was big and blacker than smoked meat; the palm of your hand could easily have gone between his two eyes; he had very large cheeks and a monstrous flat nose with great nostrils; lips redder than uncooked flesh; teeth yellow and foul; he was shod with shoes and gaiters of bull's hide, bound about the legs with ropes to well above the knee; upon his back

Corn Sacks and Store-basket.

was a rough cloak; and he stood leaning on a huge club.'

The noble's attitude to the peasants and to the town which were growing up and helping the growth of a richer peasant class, is powerfully expressed in the poems of Betran de Born, a noble of the time of Richard I:

> My heart is joyous when I see
> The cursèd rich in misery
> For baiting the nobility.

I laugh with joy to see them die,
Twenty or thirty, knee to knee,
Or when I see them, raggedly,
Come beg for bread. And if I lie,
Then my loved one lie to me.

For swine they're born and swine remain;
All decency they find a strain;
If any wealth they chance to gain,
Then all the ways of fools they try.
So keep their trough devoid of grain,
Plague them with requisitions, drain
Their pockets, and, to make them sigh,
Let them endure the wind and rain.

Hold fast the serf, or you will trace
The treason growing on his face.
That lord deserves to meet disgrace.
Who, with the chance to crush, stands by.
For peasants are a rebel race.
When sheltered in a strong-walled place
Their hearts grow insolently high,
Exposed as treacherous and base.

We can guess then how hard it was for a medieval king
and his lords to think of such people as a serious enemy
who could meet them on equal terms. But even so, it is
hard altogether to explain the inactivity of the Council
of Richard II.

That the Government had long been aware of men who
were spreading rebellious talk is shown by a Statute of
1379, two years before the revolt, which condemned

99

BATTERSEA
PUBLIC
LIBRARIES

'devisers of false news and reporters of horrible and false lies concerning prelates, dukes, earls, barons, and other nobles and great men of the realm . . . Hereof great peril and mischief might come to all the realm and quick subversion and destruction of the said realm if due remedy be not provided.' We may compare with that the charges made against John Ball by Simon Sudbury. At least some of these 'devisers of false news' must have been the wandering beggars or landless men who played their part in spreading such doctrines as Ball's.

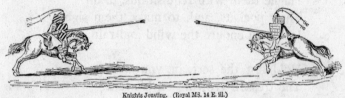

Knights Jousting. (Royal MS. 14 E. iii.)

The Council seems to have made some attempt to stop an expedition that was setting off to Portugal under the Earl of Cambridge, but the squadron had put out to sea before any orders of recall could reach the Earl. Preparations were also under way to send some small reinforcements to garrisons in Brittany. The Council countermanded the dispatch; but the only men they seem to have managed to bring under their control were the few score men-at-arms and archers whom the old soldier-of-fortune Sir Robert Knolles had enlisted. Their headquarters were in the city. Besides them there were some 600 other men, retainers of the King's Household or of the Council, who were with their masters in the Tower. A chronicler, however, tells us that they 'all had so lost heart that you would have thought them more like dead men than living; the memory of their former vigour and glory was extinguished, and in short, all the military audacity of almost the whole of the nobility 'had faded before the face of the rustics'. It seems, however, more likely that the officers did not feel that they could rely on the men for fighting against their fellow commoners.

But why did the Council not proceed to call out the gentry of the neighbouring counties, or of the Midlands, where so far the revolt had not spread? Why didn't they put under arms those sections of the London militia that Walworth told them they could trust? First, we may say that understandably they did not know whom to trust in such a rapidly deteriorating situation—and the fact that Walworth, shrewd as he was, was fooled by Horne and others, shows that they were correct enough in their fears. Secondly, we must note the enclosing ring of peasants around London, which was growing thicker all the while. The Council may well have doubted the ability of small detachments, led by lords or knights, to break through; and above all, at such a risky moment, they could not afford to have any military setbacks, which would increase the confidence of the rebels and swing large numbers of waverers over to their side. Thirdly, we may note the lack of any military head on the Council. John of Gaunt was absent on a mission to Edinburgh. Edmund of Cambridge had just sailed off to Portugal. (He must have heard alarming stories before he went, but he preferred to carry on with his own military plans rather than stay and aid the King.) Richard's uncle, Thomas of Woodstock, who had recently been responsible for a mili-

D*

tary fiasco in France and whom Richard was later to murder, was on the Welsh March.

Who was with the King in the Tower?

There was the Chancellor, Sudbury, who was in no way a man of action, and the hated Treasurer, Hales. As soon as the host appeared on Blackheath, Sudbury laid down the Great Seal and asked in fear to be allowed to withdraw from public affairs; but the Council refused to let him go.

Chair. (Royal MS. 14. E. iii.)

There were also two half-brothers of the King, the Earl of Kent and his younger brother John, a master of the tournament, with the Earls of Salisbury, Warwick, and Oxford, and the King's cousin, Henry Bolingbroke. Bolingbroke, who was later to hurl Richard from the throne, was now only about fifteen years old; and Oxford about seventeen. The Earl of Kent had been knighted by the

Black Prince during the campaign in Castile, and War-wick and Salisbury were middle-aged men, who had taken part in the French wars. Salisbury indeed had commanded, with credit, one of the wings at Poitiers; but he does not seem at this time to have been eager to shoulder any military responsibility. Nor was Sir Thomas Percy, admiral, who had been defeated in the wars at Doubise. Salisbury, however, was a shrewd man, and in the end his advice was more important to Richard than any military ardours could have been.

Let us look at the place in which these councillors sat with their king and considered the gloomy situation. The Tower in those days was no dank prison of stone, with winding stairs and draughty rooms. What remains is the White Tower—probably so called from the colour of its original stone and the coats of whitewash it was given. The White Tower was the keep; and here indeed were the council chambers, the chapel, and many offices of administration. But between it and the Thames rose a handsome palace with lodgings for king and queen, with jewel-chamber and with a great feasting-hall that stretched between the Wakefield and the Lanthorn Towers. The Council would at this time be meeting, we may be sure, amid the sumptuous surroundings of the palace.

In the city, the richer citizens seem to have been as confused and stricken as the King's Council. They knew only too well the unruly habits of commoners, their readiness to seize any chance of demonstrating against the men in power. Besides, some city councillors favoured the rebels and had done their best to hinder any vigorous measures by protesting that they were unnecessary and that Tyler was only leading a needed protest

Dining-room and Kitchen. (Harleian MS. 4375.)

against corruption and inefficiency. The Common Council, which could have called out some 5,000 well-equipped men, was so full of doubts and divisions that it did nothing.

How different things could be when any common feeling united men was shown a few years before, in 1377, when there was fear of a French attack. Then the portcullises and chains of the gates were used seriously and barbicans (outer defences) were set up. Breastworks were built along the quays. The aldermen made each inhabitant of their wards swear to be ready with his armour and to come out to fight when necessary; special taxes were imposed on innkeepers and all persons lodging in their inns; special guards were appointed at the gates;

each alderman was to be prepared to lead the men of his ward in full array; careful precautions were taken against surprise attacks at all the weak points. Further, by day no man was to wear any weapon but his baselard, though a knight might have his sword borne before him, these prohibitions being doubtless meant to prevent any disorders or armed brawls. But in the crisis of 1381 such thorough measures were impossible.

The only man who did his best to obstruct the rebels was the Lord Mayor, William Walworth, fishmonger, an unscrupulous man who came of a good Durham family. He had been apprenticed to John Lovekyn of the Fishmongers' Company ('jolly citizens', as the chronicler Stow called them), and followed his master as alderman of Bridge Ward in 1368, becoming sheriff in 1370 and mayor in 1374. Fishmongers did well in the medieval world where the Church strictly enforced the rule of nothing but fish to be eaten on Fridays and Fast Days. Fish was generally expensive: which made the fasts a burden on the poor. Walworth was rich enough to contribute £200 to the war-charges in 1370, and in 1377 Parliament made him Treasurer, with the task of seeing that the voted moneys were used for the stated purposes. He lived in the parish of St. Michael Crooked Lane (off Eastcheap); for a widow came to his house there in 1379 and 'did horribly raise the hue and cry upon the said William, as though against a thief'. She charged him with thrusting her husband into jail so that he might grab land worth £20 yearly. As a result she was condemned to be locked in the thew (the woman's pillory) with a whetstone (to sharpen her tongue) hung round her neck. But in view of the fact that we have proof of Walworth's readiness to make money by any tainted means, we may assume that she was speaking the truth. She must have known she would suffer heavily for accusing so important a citizen.

Street in London.

There is a final point to be taken into consideration in judging the King's Council's failure to act. The armies of the peasants and craftsmen were no mere hordes of disorderly civilians. The changes that Edward III had been forced to make for the effective carrying-on of his French wars had meant that a large number of commoners had been accustomed to the ways of warfare. All able-bodied men, apart from clerics, were liable to service and were trained for it. Edward had lost so many men that he was compelled to buy foreign mercenaries, but in the earlier years he drew on his own commoners. As archers, they faced the French cavalry who were enraged at the unfair English weapon which could shoot with speed and kill gentle and churl without discrimination. When in 1346 the Scots took advantage of Edward III's army being abroad, and invaded England, they were driven back by mere ploughmen and shepherds; and Sir James Douglas was so infuriated that he hacked off the right hand and put out the right eye of any captured archer.

The archer did not need any heavy armour. He wore an open helmet, with a short-sleeved mail-shirt or brigandine for his body. A leather or horn wristlet (the bracer) protected his left wrist from being chafed by the bowstring. He guarded himself against cavalry attack by driving a sharp stake into the ground in front of him; or using a big wooden shield that rested on the ground and leaned against a prop. His other weapon was a sword or a maul (a big mallet) for hand-to-hand fighting. The arrows were feathered or fledged with goose feathers, though peacock feathers were used for show; and the man who put the feathers on was a fletcher—hence the common name of Fletcher that still survives. Sheffield steel was considered the best for the heads.

In 1365 the sheriffs had been required throughout

England to issue a proclamation forbidding all able-bodied men, on pain of imprisonment, 'to meddle in hurling of stones, loggats and quoits, handball, football, club ball, cambuc, cockfighting or other vain games of no value'. Instead, on Sundays and holidays they were to practise with bows and arrows, for thus 'by God's help came forth honour to the kingdom and advantage to the King in his actions of war'. In 1388 the substance of this proclamation was made statutory, with tennis and dice added to the list of forbidden games; and this statute, with small variations was re-enacted from time to time till the sixteenth century.

Archers. (From various MSS. of the 14th Century.)

We see then that there would be no lack of trained fighters among the rebels; and there must have been many leaders who like Wat Tyler had had some experience of tactics in the French wars. And so, while counsels of doubt and indecision prevailed in the Tower, on Black-heath and at Mile End there was confident rejoicing.

Thursday 13 June was Corpus Christi, a day of solemn festival. The campers rose early to hear John Ball cele-brate Mass. For text he used the proverbial couplet:

> When Adam delved and Eve span,
> Who was then the Gentleman?

A contemporary chronicle tells us that 'by the word of that proverb which he took for his theme', he set out 'to introduce and prove that from the beginning all men were made alike by nature and that bondage and servi-tude was brought in by oppression of naughty men against the will of God. For if it had pleased God to have made bondsmen he would have appointed them from the begin-ning of the world, who should be slave and who lord. They sought to consider, therefore, that now was a time given to them by God, in the which, laying aside the con-tinual bondage, they might if they would, enjoy their long wished-for liberty.' And so he admonished them that 'they should be wise after the manner of a good husband-man that tilled the ground and did cut away all noisome weeds that were accustomed to grow and oppress the fruit, they should haste to do now at the present the like. First, the Archbishop and great men of the king-dom were to be slain. After, lawyers, justices, lastly whomsoever they knew like hereafter to be hurtful to the Commons, they should dispatch out of the land, for so they might purchase safety to themselves hereafter, if the great men being once taken away, there remained among them equal liberty, all one nobility, and like authority and power.'

The keynote of his remarks was then a demand for the equality of all men before the law and for the ending of serfdom. The sheriff who later inquired into the event said that the sermon made 'the common people to esteem of him in such a manner' that they cried out 'he should be Archbishop of Canterbury and Chancellor of the realm, for he only deserved the honour'. The sermon is of importance in stating plainly what were the main ideas of Wat Tyler and the other leaders of the revolt; for on such an important occasion—a moment that was both the high crest of the uprising and a solemn religious festival (when there were normally great processions through the streets)—Ball would clearly make a carefully considered statement that both summed up his own teaching and expressed the agreed aims of the rebels. He made an outright challenge to all the dominant ideas of Church and State, which taught that nature and God alike had instituted the different social degrees as eternal things; the right order for the world had been achieved for all time and any attempts to change it were condemned from the outset, whatever they were. Ball on the contrary insisted that the differences in rank had not always existed and had been brought about by the actions of men which outraged the original equality of all in work, as exemplified by Adam digging and Eve spinning, both equal in the eyes of God.

Such ideas were not only challenging to the feudal world with its belief that change in itself was a bad thing; they seemed to the men who dominated that world a rank madness, something that the mind could not even grasp, let alone accept. Even the King, though considered semi-divine, could not approach God as an equal; he had to use the mediating clergy, among whom difference of rank was an essential thing. Ball with his doctrine of equality before God and the law seemed to men with feudal minds to be crazed and driven by devils. The Earl of Salisbury, on hearing of Ball's words, cried out that if the rebels succeeded, 'It will be all over with us and our heirs, and England will be a desert.'

After the Mass with its sermon that laid down the policy of the uprising, Wat Tyler presided over a meeting of the leaders. A message to the King was worked out and was sent by one of the hostages, a knight; Alderman Horne was again present. He told the rebel council that all preparations were now concluded in the city. 'Come to London,' he said, 'we are all to a man your friends and ready to act with you as you have suggested, and to show you obedience.'

The message that was taken to the King by the hostage set out in forthright terms the popular discontents. For years the kingdom had been misgoverned, to the great dishonour of the realm and to the great oppression of the people, both by the King's uncle, John of Gaunt, and by the clergy, especially the Archbishop of Canterbury, from whom the uprisen people were resolved to extort an account of his ministry.

As soon as the knight entered the Tower, he was conducted into the presence of the King and the Court. Among the councillors surrounding the throne were Walworth and other big merchants, who were frightened at the development of the rebellion. Joan of Kent, the King's mother, was also there. She was his guardian, a

Street in London: Cheapside.

strong-minded woman who played her part in the discussion of policy and who had dominated her son. He showed himself later an unstable character, given to hasty actions and sudden bursts of emotion, a stammerer who could fall into deep depressions; a luxury-lover, who had no powers of self-discipline, at times crafty and revengeful, but lacking the capacity to sustain any policy with effect. It is highly unlikely that as a boy he played any part in the deliberations of the Council during these dangerous days.

The knight began with humble apologies for appearing as the messenger of rebels. He protested that he was a prisoner who had been constrained to carry a message that he detested.

The councillors were not however in the least interested in his fears and qualms. He was promptly bidden by Richard, 'Tell us what you are charged with, we hold you excused.'

The knight then repeated his message, adding, 'They wish to have no one but yourself and you need not fear for your person, as they will not do you the least harm. They have always respected you as their King and will continue to do so. But they desire to tell you many things which they say it is necessary that you should hear.'

The councillors were very relieved at these words. At last they saw something on which they could base their policy. They had the King as their bargaining counter, and if they used him shrewdly they could set up various delays and at last baffle the rebels. But not all of them fully understood how to use the one advantage they held. Sudbury and Hales took the line that it was beneath the King's dignity to meet with 'shoeless ruffians' who dared to criticize matters that were no concern of theirs. But men like Salisbury had subtler minds. They realized that in such an exposed position they must seem to bow to the storm; nothing must be done to make the people fear that they could not reach and affect the King. Once the people lost the belief that the King could be won over and removed from evil counsellors, they would make a clean sweep of the whole system of lordships, or they would begin slaughtering the lords as the French peasants had recently done in their Jacquerie.

It was therefore decided that the people must be humoured. The King must deign to visit them as if he were really ready to consider their grievances.

So, next morning the royal barge was seen coming out from the Tower, followed by four others. It moved down the river to Rotherhithe. With Richard were Sudbury, the Earls of Warwick, Salisbury, and Oxford, and others of the Council. As the King's barge neared the thickly crowded slopes, Richard and his ministers were given a chance to grasp the vast extent of the rebellion. Some 10,000 men stood there in polished steel, holding aloft two great banners and some forty pennons; and no doubt there was an indistinguishable mass gathered on the Essex shore, to watch from afar.

'When the King and his lords saw this crowd of people and the wildness of their manner,' we are told, 'there was not one among them so bold and determined but felt alarmed.'

The barges took care to keep well away from the shore, coming within some twenty yards, then feathering oars or backing a safe distance. A huge tumult broke out. Some men gave cheers for the King; others yelled for the heads of John of Gaunt and Sudbury; yet others brandished their weapons and simply shouted. Tyler and the other leaders waited respectfully; but the sight of the hated lords was too much for many of the men. However in a lull the King raised his voice to open the parley. 'Sirs, what do you want? Tell me, now that I have come to talk with you.'

The crowd shouted back that he must come ashore, they had many things to say, they couldn't confer with him at a distance. But to land would have meant putting

Richard II. and Gower.

the King at the mercy of the rebels. They would certainly have behaved courteously, indeed rejoicingly, at
finding him among them; but they might have been temp-
ted to attack the lords—or to put them back into the
barge and tell them to return to the Tower. The latter
course would have been equally disastrous to the cause of
the lords; for it would have cut the King off and enabled
the rebels to act in his name without chance of being
contradicted.

Salisbury called out to the peasants, 'Gentlemen, you
are not properly dressed, nor in fit condition for the King
to talk with you.'

The peasants answered with another roar; and Salisbury or Sudbury, or both of them, ordered the bargemen

to retreat and make haste back to the Tower. The peasants burst into curses and shouts of 'Treason!' But they did not send a flight of arrows after the barge. If they had wanted, they could have killed everyone on board.

The obvious respect with which they had treated Richard heartened the Council and confirmed what the knight-messenger had said. It became ever clearer that there lay the one strong weapon they held in what was for the moment the extremely unequal and hazardous task of fooling and defeating Wat Tyler and his host.

CHAPTER 8

THE PEASANTS ENTER LONDON

TYLER realized that nothing was to be gained by such inconclusive parleys. While the King remained in the Tower inside an untaken London, no advance could be made. At all costs the rebels must enter London. Though the peasants in general had shown good military order in their movements, there was no organized commissariat; the problem of feeding such a large body of men was acute. They had already eaten up their short supplies of food: what they had brought with them and what they could get from the villages south of the Thames. The London sheriffs in their later report declared that before long the host would have had to disperse through hunger and that they were already talking about the need to return home.

Tyler must have been well aware also of the difficulty of holding big bands of peasants indefinitely together. The lords held their retainers by paying wages. The peasants had hurried from their holdings with all sorts of jobs left half done or undone, and with more jobs needing to be done there every day that they wandered afield. Such men could not be expected to stay on cam-

paigning like a normal army. For a peasant revolt to succeed, it must be able to strike quickly and attain its ends.
If it was caught up in a situation of long delays and un-
certainties, it must break down; more and more men
would daily go off to their homes.

Tyler gave the word for the advance on London.

As the host moved into Southwark and approached
London Bridge, Alderman Horne rode up. He waved a
standard with the royal arms which he had managed to
obtain from the town clerk by false pretences. He harangued the men, bidding them press on, for they would
find no one but friends in London.

What he said was true enough; for the Billingsgate
Alderman, Walter Sybyle, who had charge of the drawbridge, was on the side of the attackers. When royalist
burgesses had come to offer him their aid and to streng-
then the bridge's garrison, he told them angrily to go
away, mind their own business, and leave him to do his
duty in his own ward. Now he heard the peasants ap-
proaching and smiled. The Stone Gate, the southern en-
trance to the bridge, was a strong structure, which Walworth had done his best to fortify further, protecting it
with a heavy iron chain. On the landward side of it
stood some twenty shops—ten a side—and stables.

Tyler now sent word that unless the drawbridge was
instantly lowered, he would set fire to the whole bridge
and burn it down, while his army crossed the Thames in
boats. Sybyle then gave orders for the drawbridge to be
let down, the chain removed, and the gate opened. The
rebels, some 30,000 strong, poured across the bridge. The
cobbled passage was narrow, lined on each side by shops
that sometimes met overhead and made a dark tunnel.

Street in London.

About the same time, on the other side of the city, Alderman Tonge admitted the Essex men, to whom had been added contingents from Hertfordshire, Suffolk, and Cambridgeshire. The gate which he opened was Aldgate on the north. 'But whether he was in agreement with the aforesaid John Horne and Walter Sybyle, or because he was terrified by the threats of the Kentish rebels, who had already entered the city, no man knows to this day.' Heading the Essex army were Thomas Farringdon and Jack Straw.

The entries of the two armies were orderly and disciplined. 'They entered in troops,' says Froissart, 'of one or two hundred, by twenties or thirties, according to the populousness of the towns they came from.' Even the most antagonistic of the chroniclers agree that there was no wild behaviour, no plundering. Tyler had issued strict orders against all theft; and his captains, warning persons who were not members of the rebel armies and who might try to seize the chance for loot, declared, 'We are zealots for Truth and Justice, not thieves and robbers.' All supplies which were set at their disposal were duly paid for, unless they were expressly offered as gifts. The crowds lining the streets cheered the marchers, as the citizens of Canterbury had done. Then, once the men had been lodged according to plan, various detachments were led off by London partisans to carry out their allotted tasks.

Records of the period tell us what the members of the London militia who joined the rebels would have been wearing. An order of August the year before says, 'Precept was sent to each alderman to see that the men of his ward were suitably armed with basinet (a kind of light helmet), gauntlets of plate, habergeon (a sleeveless mail-coat), sword, dagger and hatchet, according to their estate, and inferior men arrayed with good bows, arrows, sword, and buckler.'

By the afternoon of Thursday 13 June the rebels had complete control of London without striking a single blow. Apprentices and journeymen were rushing everywhere to welcome the rebels, clap them on the backs, and listen to their stories and songs. The girls were peeping at them from the upper windows or the alleys. Even the smaller merchants were giving them friendly words. The great city was all theirs.

Large numbers of the peasants could never have seen it before. They would have been awed by its huddled size, its dark twisting lanes, its splendid places with orchards and gardens, its noble monastic edifices and its mob of churches with their variously clanging bells, its long cobbled streets, its painted and gilt houses with slanting roofs of red tiles, its great bishop's palace at the north-west corner of St. Paul's. Cheapside was the centre with its big cross and its two water-conduits, with the space so broad that tournaments were held there—though now it would be divided across by moveable sheds or booths called 'selds'. The goldsmiths congregated here in their richly carved and shuttered houses and there were so many taverns that a few years before complaints had been made about

Club-ball. (From a MS. in Bodleian Collection, and Royal MS. 14 B 4.)

their alestakes or signs. These stuck out so far as to get in the way of riders and were so heavy as to damage the houses to which they were fixed. So an order was issued to the taverners that any signs projecting more than seven feet would bring a fine of forty pence at the Guildhall. In the evening, in Westcheap and on Cornhill, there were special markets held often by candlelight, so that many thefts occurred and cheats were practised.

Normally the streets with shops were loud with the voices of apprentices, with clubs in their belts, praising their masters' wares and trying to pull passers-by inside. A poet of the period, Gower, cites them calling by the mercers' shops, 'Come in, come in! Beds and kerchiefs, ostrich feathers, silks and satins and imported cloths, come, I'll give you a look at them, for if you're thinking of buying you needn't go any farther, here is the best in the street.' The poem, *London Lickpenny*, tells of men yelling 'Hot peascods' and 'Strawberries ripe', and offering pepper and saffron.

> Then to Cheapside I went on,
> Where much people I saw for to stand.
> One offered me velvet, silk, and lawn;
> Another he takes me by the hand,
> 'Here is Paris thread, the finest in the land.'
> I never was used to such things indeed,
> And wanting money, I might not speed.
>
> Then I went forth by London Stone,
> Throughout all Candlewick Street;
> Drapers much cloth offered me anon.
> Then met I one, cried, 'Hot sheep's feet.'

One cried, 'Mackerel.' 'Rushes green,' another
   gan greet.
One bade me buy a hood to cover my head;
But for want of money I might not speed.

Then I hied me into Eastcheap.
One cried, 'Ribs of beef and many a pie.'
Pewter-pots they clattered on a heap;
There was harp, pipe, and minstrelsy.
'Yea, by Cock!' 'Nay, by Cock!' some began cry;
Some sang of Jenken and Julian for their need,
But for lack of money I might not speed.

Then into Cornhill I took my road,
Where was much stolen goods among;
I saw where hung my own hood
That I had lost among the throng
To buy my own hood I thought it wrong,
I knew it well as I did my creed,
But for lack of money I could not speed.

Bowling-Ball. (From a MS. in the Douce Collection.)

The streets were usually not very clean, though rakers were employed to take away the worst of the rubbish. Slops were thrown out of windows and garbage collected in the draining gutter that ran down the middle of most streets. From time to time orders were issued to householders, bidding them remove nuisances or pave the street before their places when it had become dangerously full of holes and lumps. The city also levied various tolls, for instance, on goods coming in at the wharfs or ports between the Bridge and the Wool Quay, or on rushes and straw being brought in for floor-coverings; and used the proceeds to pave or clean the streets. There was the threat of a 4d. fine to induce householders to clear muck from their doorsteps; but much of the worst offal was removed by carrion-birds.

There were many rotting hovels as well as handsome merchant houses. These, if more than one storey high, had the staircase outside, and the upper-storey stuck out, darkening the narrow alleys. The porters of the city gates were instructed to keep a watch out for lepers and prevent them from entering London; and a law of 1359 threatened beggars with the Cornhill pillory and with forty days' jail for a third conviction. The number of poor people is shown by the tumults at the distribution of alms. Nine men and women were trampled to death in a rush in 1315, and fifty-five in 1322.

Taverns and aleshops abounded. Hops had not yet come in for brewing, and ale was made only of malt: 1½d. a gallon for the best kind, 1d. a gallon for inferior ones. Wines were more expensive, and there were many complaints of vintners cheating, selling cider for Rhenish wine or various dregs in a pitch-lined cask for Romany. Water was often contaminated and dangerous to drink; so ale was the usual drink for everyone. By 1309, London, with some 30,000 people, had 354 taverns and 1,334 beer-houses. Bakers had their mills outside the city bounds and sent in apprentices to hawk loaves about. People also had their own bread baked in bakers' ovens. At least one baker had a hole cut in the table on which they put their dough, with an apprentice underneath to scoop out a few handfuls of dough as it lay there.

Passage of the Host. Cripples worshipping.—(Cotton MS. Nero, D. 1.)

The price of goods and the rate of wages or rents keep on coming up into our story; but it is hard to compare these with modern prices or rates. Clearly money had in general a very much higher purchasing power than in our world; but at the same time we must realize that people, especially in the country, made much less use of money at all than we do. Some idea of the relative positions may be gained by looking at some lists of prices of the later fourteenth century.

E

Thus in a haberdasher's shop in 1378 we find a red cap costing 7d.; 2 loose shirts of hair, 1s.; a white hat, 3d.; 6 purses of red leather, 4d.; 4 eyeglasses, 2s.; 2 wooden coffers, 8d.; a pair of children's boots of white woollen cloth, 2d.; 18 inkhorns, 1s. 6d. In a cook shop of 1378, the best roast pig 8d.; the best roast lamb, 7d.; the best roast hen, 4d.; 3 roast pigeons, 2½d.; 10 eggs, 1d. And a shopkeeper might have a very small stock. One who struck a midnight reveller and killed him in 1322 had his goods valued at 6s. 11½d., 2 small pigs at 3s. making up the main part, with a broken chest and a table worth 6d. and a pair of worn linen sheets worth 4d.

Library Chair, Reading Table, and Reading Desk.
(Royal MS. 15 D. iii.)

Now the rebel army was in London, and they set about what they conceived to be necessary actions. They marched through London till they came to Fleet Street. There they broke open the Fleet Prison and freed the prisoners. After that they turned to the Temple, the lawyers' centre. In this hated place the peasants did their best to wreck the houses, to pull off the tiles and crash the structures down. So disliked were the lawyers in the medieval world that even a chronicler cannot hide his satisfaction at the disasters come upon them. He writes, 'It was marvellous to see how even the most aged and infirm of the lawyers scrambled off with the agility of rats or evil spirits.'

The Temple had become the headquarters of the lawyers of England. Here were their inns, schools, and library. The rebels broke open all the chests, and destroyed vast numbers of charters, muniments, and records. They broke up the chests and used the wood as fuel for the bonfires. The library was in the Temple Church, as in Oxford the University books were kept at St. Mary's.

The Temple belonged to the Knights Hospitallers of St. John who had taken it over from the Knights Templars when the latter were crushed and expropriated by the Church; and the head of the Hospitallers in England was the King's Treasurer, Hales, Hob the Robber. There was thus a further reason for the peasants' animosity towards the Temple. But they did not forget Hales himself. Farringdon led a detachment of Essex men to the Priory of St. John in Clerkenwell, where the church hospital and the home of the Hospitallers were burnt. Also, seven Flemings who had taken refuge there, were dragged from the altar and killed. This action must have been the work of London craftsmen and had nothing to do with the aims of the revolt.

But the main action was being taken against the most hated man in the kingdom, John of Gaunt, whose great

Hoodman Blind. (Bodleian MS.)

mansion, in his manor of the Savoy, was the most magnificent private residence to be found. It had only recently been finished and was stored with all kinds of valuables, tapestries, carpets, painted chests, rich furniture, fine armour and clothes, plate, rare ornaments and jewellery —gifts of his father Edward III and the loot of France. There was a noble garden running down to the river. (In 1372 the gardener, by name Nicholas Gardener, who was paid 2d. a day, was given the right to use the herbs and fruits that were not needed by the household. Nicholas was to work the gardens at his own cost and provide everything needed for the work except any rails and rods 'for the time of paling'.)

With shouts of 'To the Savoy!' the rebels moved on westward. They reached the manor about 4 o'clock. All guards and servants had long since slipped away. Tyler had issued strict orders that the mansion and its contents were to be destroyed as tokens of oppression, but that nothing was to be stolen. On arrival the rebels set about their task methodically. The doors were broken in. All the articles in the house were thrown out into the street to be hacked to bits and piled high for burning, pounded up with big hammers and thrown into the Thames. Jewels were smashed to dust. One rogue was detected trying to sidle off with a silver goblet. He was at once hanged. However, a small group of Rochester men managed to smuggle out Gaunt's strongbox with £1,000 in it. They got it down to the riverside and carried it by boat across to Southwark, where they divided up the contents. (In 1382, John Farrour and his wife Joanna were indicted for the theft.)

Finally, three barrels of gunpowder from the duke's armoury were brought out and the building was fired. The huge crowd stood watching at a safe distance till the barrels exploded and completed the work of the fire. Some drunkards who had crept into the cellars to tap the casks there were blown up. The flames went on flaring and flickering till late at night.

The Savoy.

Here, and elsewhere, the rebels seem to have started off no unwanted fires in a city where the crowded buildings made the spreading of fires dangerously easy. Usually in London during the hot time of the year the aldermen were required to see that a large vessel of water stood outside each house for use in fire-fighting, that ladders and hooks (for pulling down a place on fire) were kept ready, and that good access in general was provided for getting at any fire that might break out; and special precautions were taken to ensure that all taverns and houses of brewers were shut up by 10 o'clock in the evening. The fact that London was not burned down in the excited and tumultuous days of its occupation by the rebels shows that Tyler maintained a strong discipline.

While the peasants and their London sympathizers were watching the embers of Gaunt's mansion, wandering boisterously in the streets, or sitting down for a friendly exchange of ideas and experiences, Wat Tyler and his lieutenants were meeting in the house of Farringdon. There they drew up their plans for the next day, formulating their demands in full, and making a list of the men considered to merit execution for their misdeeds against the people. This list included John of Gaunt, Sudbury, Hales, the Bishop of London, the Clerk of the Privy Seal (who was bishop-elect of Durham), the Chief Justice Belknap, the Chief Baron, Sir Ralph Ferrers, John Legge, the King's serjeant who had advised sending out the poll-tax commissioners, Thomas Bampton, and the sub-treasurer of the realm.

The demands which were worked out so that they might be set before the King at the first opportunity, ran as follows: (1) that all men should be free from servitude and bondage so that henceforth there should be no bondsmen; (2) that the King should pardon all men of what estate soever, all manner of actions and insurrections committed and all manner of treasons, felonies, transgressions and extortions by any of them done, and to grant them peace; (3) that all men might henceforth be enfranchised to buy and sell in every county, city, borough, town, fair, market, and other place within the realm of England; (4) that no acre of land holden in bondage or service should be holden out but for 4d.; and if it had been holden for less aforetime, it should not be hereafter enhanced.

Briefly, these demands may be summed up as: freedom from serfdom, freedom of trade, easing of the conditions on which land was held, and common justice.

The first proposal simply stated that the rebels wanted the end of all forms of servitude and bondage. By granting it, the King would free all the serfs on the soil of England. The farmer and labourer could not be compelled to work for a lord without wages or pay him fines for the ordinary business of living. The man who had been a serf was to have the same rights as the freeman—that is, he was to have legal rights against his lord in the King's Courts of Law.

The second proposal ensured that when the peasants laid down arms on their return home, they would not be open to all sorts of prosecutions for their actions committed before the King granted the new system of rights. Since the aims of their rebellion would have been accepted by the King and incorporated in his law, they were not to be prosecuted for the steps they had taken in bringing this situation about.

The third proposal ensured a general freedom of buying and selling. No longer would the lord be able to enforce his many monopolies, nor would the privileges gained by various boroughs be used to make trade between countryman and townsman profitable to the latter at the expense of the former.

The fourth proposal meant that the poor peasant would have his land freed from all the customary dues, fines, and services that had burdened it. He wanted the King to commute all the burdens to an inclusive rate of 4d. per acre. (The rents paid by the richer peasants, which might go as high as 2s. per acre, represented the efforts made by the lords to get as high a value as they could for their lands. No doubt the farmers paying these higher rents, who also widely supported the rebellion, felt that they could use the grievances of the poorer tenants to bring down the charges of their own leasehold land.)

We may note first that the four points showed a carefully considered policy and were the work of men who had thought long and deep about the situation in England. They were in no way a wildly improvised programme. And secondly we may note that in fact they forecast with complete precision the course of history. All the demands of the peasants were to be met in due time during the next centuries; and if they had not been met, England could never have developed into a modern country as it has done. The men who had a clear and correct vision of the way that history should move were Wat Tyler and the peasants he led. The men who had a clouded view, unable to realize what was humanly and historically needed because of their personal and social prejudices, were the lords, secular and ecclesiastic, who saw only anarchy, confusion, and the end of civilized existence, in the demands of the peasants.

Wat Tyler and his council must also have gone on to weigh up the situation. They held the capital, London, and the main towns of Kent and Essex, and controlled all the roads leading in. The rebellion was sweeping out in all directions. Clearly East Anglia, Cambridgeshire, Hertfordshire, and other areas would be in full revolt in a few days if they were not already so. There were no signs of any force being mustered to relieve the hopelessly beleaguered King's Council.

On the other hand, there were the many acute problems of keeping a peasant army in the field. For the moment the capture of London had removed all difficulties of finding food and lodging. But the peasants could not remain in the capital indefinitely. They would end by outstaying their welcome and would begin to worry about their homes, their families, and the work to be done on the land. Further, the army-chest of the rebels could not be large.

Clearly it was necessary to settle things as soon as possible. The demands must be pressed on the King. The most must be made of the demoralized condition of his Council, to draw him over into a full acceptance of the rebels' programme, and to detach him from the advisers who had so far dominated him. He must be prepared to accept Wat Tyler and John Ball as his settled counsellors.

Inside the Tower, no doubt in the keep, another conference was going on, with the fires of the Savoy lurid in the windows and with noisy rebels encamping around. Camp-fires were blazing and every now and then there were shouts for the heads of traitors. In this depressing

E*

The Tower in the 15th Century.

situation the King's Council put their heads together and tried to find some source of comfort. No doubt, if they had known London would fall without a blow and the mass of the citizens would side with the rebels, they would have retired with the King to the Midlands before the city was surrounded—before the Kentishmen had swarmed into Blackheath.

But such a withdrawal was now impossible. Two opposing lines of policy distracted the Council. Some of its members said that desperate measures were needed. Let the men-at-arms make a midnight sally against the rebels and rout them before they could organize their defence. The disorderly crowd could be cleft through by an attack of the experienced and hardy soldiers. The Lord Mayor, Walworth, was keen for violent action. He insisted that even now he could guarantee that some 6,000 to 7,000 well-armed men from the households of the wealthy citizens would hurry out to support any such sally. Sir Robert Knolles with his compact body of men-at-arms would provide the nucleus of the attack.

But the Earl of Salisbury was against any such risky scheme. He thought that a sally might at first have the desired effect. But if the rebels rallied and were joined by the London craftsmen, as they would certainly be, then the whole thing would become disastrous. Street-fighting would develop. The salliers would be crushed by weight of numbers in difficult situations where their skill and their drive would be useless. They would be unable to hold together and might well be cut to pieces in small groups.

'If we begin what we cannot carry through, we shall never be able to repair matters,' said Salisbury.

That was the crucial point. Once the councillors came out from behind the King and had recourse to battle, they could not afford the least defeat. They would be wiped out and Richard would fall into the hands of the rebels.

Salisbury therefore wanted to protract things as long as possible. 'Sire,' he continued to the King, 'if we can appease them by fair words and grant them what they wish, it will be so much the better.' His scheme was to promise anything as long as the promises got the peasants to disperse. Promises could always be taken back, but no headway could be made while the peasants remained under arms, with a resolute leader like Wat Tyler.

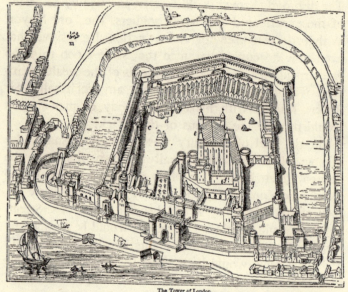

The Tower of London.

From a Print published by the Royal Antiquarian Society, and engraved from the Survey made in 1597, by W. Haiward and J. Gascoigne, by order of Sir J. Peyton, Governor of the Tower.—*a*, Lion's Tower; *b*, Bell Tower; *c*, Beauchamp Tower; *d*, The Chapel; *e*, Keep, called also Cæsar's, or the White Tower; *f*, Jewel House; *g*, Queen's Lodgings; *h*, Queen's Gallery and Garden; *i*, Lieutenant's Lodgings; *k*, Bloody Tower; *l*, St. Thomas's Tower (now Traitor's Gate); *m*, Place of Execution on Tower Hill.

Down below, outside the Tower, the peasants were singing and talking around their camp-fires, polishing their weapons and laughing. 'At times,' says Froissart, 'these rebellious fellows hooted as loud as if the devils were in them.' And devils indeed their rough shouts and merriment must have sounded to the great men trying to work out a policy by guttering candlelight.

Among the tales that were told, we may be sure that an old legend came up, telling how when the Tower barbican was being built, a passing priest saw the ghost of an archbishop holding a cross on high. The ghost was staring wrathfully at the building, with his dead clerk standing behind him. 'Why build ye these?' cried the ghost to the masons and struck with his cross at the walls so that they broke up and fell into the river, leaving only a wreath of smoke. The priest, awed, whispered to the ghostly clerk, asking his master's name. The clerk replied, 'St. Thomas the Martyr'—that is, Becket with his revered tomb at Canterbury. Why had he destroyed the barbican? The priest then asked. 'St. Thomas,' said the clerk, 'by birth a citizen, dislikes these works because they are raised in scorn and against the public right. For this cause he has thrown them down beyond the tyrant's power to restore them.'

Salisbury's plan was accepted; and it was decided to make a first attempt at conciliatory promises at once. Richard went up on to a turret or bastion looking down on St. Katharine's wharf. He gazed at the swarming and exultant rebels. Then a herald at his side blew a trumpet and called on the men below to disperse and return peacefully to their homes. If they obeyed, no one would be punished for actions done during the rebellion, and the King would look into their grievances.

The people shouted back with one voice that they would not go home till they had the traitors in the Tower in their hands and till they were given charters of freedom from all villeinage.

The King called for pen and ink, and ordered a clerk to write out a Bill. In it he thanked the people for their loyalty, pardoned all misdemeanours so far committed, ordered the host to return home, and promised that he and his Council would provide such remedies as would be for the good of the realm.

A Herald reading his Despatches.

Two knights then took the Bill down and made their way to the wharf. Consent was given by the captains for the Bill's reading, but the knights found that they could not see to read in the darkness. Torches were produced and somebody carried along an old chair. While the King and his councillors watched eagerly and anxiously from above, one of the knights climbed carefully up on to the creaking chair. Then, while the torches burned red-green and spat out their resin, he read out Richard's offer. The people pressed in round him, thick lines of them dimly visible outside the patch of smoky light.

When he had finished, a great shout came. 'All this is trifles and mockery!'

The captain-in-charge told the knight to return to the King and inform him that the people were determined to have their demands met in full before laying down their arms.

But before he had returned with this message, the councillors knew that the scheme had failed and that they would not be able to fob the peasants off with vague and general promises. After further discussion they decided that the only thing was for the King to meet the rebels face to face and to agree to whatever specific demands were made. They chose as the place, Mile End, where the Essex men were encamped, a mile or two from the Tower outside the city walls. Mile End was a village with meadows used for festivities, a favourite suburban promenade of the London citizens. No doubt there were several reasons for choosing the site. The Essex men would be there and the mass of the other rebels would certainly march out to see the exciting event. That would mean London largely evacuated by the rebels, and perhaps for a moment Walworth put forward hopes of the royalists in the city seizing the gates and shutting the rebels out. In the open space, anyhow, the royal party would not feel so perilously hemmed in as if they faced the embattled people inside London. Perhaps the exodus would give Sudbury, Hales, Legge, and other marked characters a chance to flee.

So Mile End was chosen as the meeting-place and a message was sent to Wat Tyler and the other leaders stating that Richard would confer with them there on the morrow.

CHAPTER 9

CONFERENCE AT MILE END

———

On Friday 14 June at 7 a.m. the King left the Tower for the rendezvous. He seems to have been rather afraid, as was indeed to be expected of so young a ruler in so complex and difficult a situation. A reliable chronicler of the same time says, 'The King rode timidly to the place of meeting, like a lamb among wolves seemed he, as one in great dread of his life, and he meekly entreated the people standing about.' Sudbury and Hales had been left behind, as certain to raise the wrath of the people and thus frustrate Salisbury's plans; but the rest of the court was there, even Joan of Kent, the King's mother. She may well have been brought along to keep a watch on her son and to make sure that he acted his allotted part with effect. She travelled in a whirlecote, a sort of carriage.

A menacing start had been given to the day on Tower Hill. Farringdon grasped the King's bridle. He had come from guiding Jack Straw to the Highbury mansion of Hales as the Prior of the Hospitallers, which was to be fired and was in an excited frame of mind. 'Avenge me on that false traitor the Prior,' he cried, 'who has deprived me of my tenements by fraud. Do me right justice and give me back my own. For if you do not give me back my own, I am strong enough now to take justice into my own hands.'

Richard replied that he should have all that was just.

Farringdon then left the King and joined the ranks of the men detailed to stay behind and keep up the blockade of the Tower. There he waited for further instructions according to the results of the conference at Mile End.

A little farther on along the route, a rebel named William Trewman labouring under some personal grievance, stopped the horse of an ex-mayor of London, Nicholas Brembre who rode in the royal retinue. He loaded Brembre with insults and was held back with some difficulty from assaulting him. Such episodes must have increased the sense of insecurity in the King and his men.

Half-Groat of Richard II.

Among the notables were Warwick, Oxford, Kent, Sir Thomas Holland, Sir Thomas Percy, Sir Richard Knolles, and the Lord Mayor. The sword of state was borne before Richard by the Earl of Oxford's uncle, Aubrey de Vere. All the way from the Tower to Mile End the cavalcade had to ride between thick crowds of silently and suspiciously watching rebels, who stared at their bright coats and mantles, their velvet caps and long-tailed shoes. The nobles must have ridden carefully, for the least mistake that roused the emotions of the crowd might have led to an attack. If a group of distraught or specially embittered rebels had raised an outcry and flung stones or shot arrows, there might well have resulted a massacre in which the King would be knocked over and trampled.

But Tyler had given strict orders that no one was to interfere with the King and his retinue; and his word was obeyed. (It was lucky for the King and the lords that John of Gaunt was absent; for if he had been in London this June, he could not have been omitted from the royal party and his hated presence might have been too much for the people to bear.)

Indeed, the sight of the grim faces of the onlookers was so unnerving that the King's two half-brothers, the Earl of Kent and Sir John Holland, managed to edge their horses away from the royal party. Then, when they were sufficiently distant, they turned off and galloped away over the fields to Whitechapel.

However, at last Mile End was reached. Here, on the pastures with their few farmhouses, the rebel army was drawn up in battle-order under two banners of St. George. As the royal party came near, the men greeted them with shouts for King Richard and the True Commons. They fell on their knees and welcomed the King.

A detachment headed by Wat Tyler then came forward and made two requests. Firstly, that the rebels be allowed to seize all traitors to the King throughout the country and execute them. Secondly, that the King would grant the petitions they wished to present and which they had ready in writing. (The freeing of all prisoners was probably a third proviso.)

When, however, Wat stated bluntly, 'The Commons will

that you suffer them to take and deal with all the traitors who have sinned against you and the law,' the King hesitated and began to give evasive answers.

Any such, he assured Wat, who could be proved traitors, would be arrested and punished by law.

Wat, however, insisted on a more definite reply; and after some fencing, Richard surrendered and agreed that the rebels should be free to deal as they wished with the men whom they defined as enemies of the people—men such as the ministers lurking in the Tower. He was carrying out as well as he could the policy which Salisbury had formulated—at all costs the rebels were to be humoured and made to think that they could get their programme accepted by him.

Tyler put his clauses one by one.

Richard agreed to the abolition of serfdom over all the realm, the ending of all feudal services, the commutation of all holders in villeinage into free tenants paying the moderate rent of 4d. per acre. All restrictions on buying and selling were to cease, and the amnesty for all irregularities committed during the uprising was to be granted.

Richard humbly acquiesced. He promised to give his banner to the chosen representative of each county present, as a sign that he had taken them directly under his protection. And as a proof of the sincerity of his promises, he engaged to set thirty clerks drawing up charters that would confer the amnesty and freedom on the folk of all districts coming forward to claim them. The clerks indeed got quickly to work, perhaps even at Mile End. For a large number of documents were issued that day and the formula is preserved in more than one copy:

Know that of our special grace we have manumitted all our liege and singular subjects and others of the county of Hertford, freed each and all of their old bondage, and made them quit by these presents; pardoned them all felonies, treasons, transgressions, and extortions committed by any and all of them, and assure them of our *summa pax* [highest or supreme peace].

The demands drawn up in Farringdon's house were thus fully granted. There seems no doubt that Richard, in generally accepting whatever the rebels asked, approved of the repeal of the Statue of Labourers; for one of the demands stated that no man henceforth was to serve another but of his own free will and for wages, by mutual consent.

Finally, after all the demands had been stated and accepted, Richard asked Wat Tyler to draw up his army in two long lines. He then rode slowly along the ranks, while a herald proclaimed the concessions he had made and his promise that all 'traitors' should be punished.

All the rebels were jubilant. They felt certain that they had now won. They should, however, have been suspicious at the suddenness and completeness of the King's surrender. Apart from his slight hesitations about the 'traitors', he had agreed to their demands without the least demur and in effect had made them his legal Government as if nothing more was involved than a change of ministers. He had admitted that he had been badly counselled and guided, and that from now on he would recognize the True Commons as his sole advisers. The leaders of the Commons, Tyler, Ball, and the others, thus in effect became the King's Council. The economic as well as the political power of the lords was brought down; for the 4d. rent would not suffice for their feudal grandeur, lavish way of living, costly arms, and large bodies of retainers who did no productive work.

Bowling.

The rebels might accordingly consider themselves now to be the only legal force in the land. But according to immemorial tradition, the King was bound by customary usage, by the decisions of Parliament and by the words of his Council. So, on the basis of custom—the strongest court of appeal in the medieval world—the King would have the right to repudiate all the grants, charters, and concessions, if ever he again was able to free himself from the control of the rebels.

Some at least of the rebels must have understood their weak constitutional position. The fact that they did not at once all disperse after Mile End proved that they felt their work was still not completed. Men like Wat Tyler and John Ball could have had no illusions about the lords surrounding the King, and could not have believed, that until the power of those lords had been thoroughly broken there would be any security in the grants of freedom.

But some blind spot in their outlook, something that still tethered them to the feudal world and its preconceptions, must have held them back from grasping the full logic of their position and acting on it.

They could only have been safe if, after gaining their concessions, they had turned to the King and said, 'It is now clear, sire, that you must at once get rid of all your present councillors, who are compromised one way or another with the policy that you renounce. The test of your sincerity in granting the charters can lie only in your appointing Wat Tyler, John Ball, and other known leaders of the people as your ministers, and in putting yourself personally into their charge.'

But a lingering respect for the consecrated King as a semi-divine being prevented them from taking this obvious step. They must have meant to take it sooner or later, or there could have been nothing stable about the new England that they hoped to found; but in their joy at having apparently gained acceptance for their main demands from the King, they felt reluctant to put on him the final pressure which alone could safeguard those demands. They cheered him and let him go with his lords and courtiers.

While the clerks were copying out the charters for the various groups of rebels, Wat conferred with local leaders who wanted his advice. In particular he discussed the situation in St. Albans with Will Grindcobbe, the leader of the townsfolk there. At the news of the march on London, Grindcobbe, together with some of his followers, had set out to meet Wat. On Friday 14 June he came across the band led by Jack Straw, who were destroying Hales's mansion at Highbury. The two bands mingled on the heights overlooking London, and the men of St. Albans took the rebel oath. On reaching Mile End, Grindcobbe witnessed the King's surrender and then went to report to Wat Tyler. Wat promised him full support and said that if the forces of the Abbot of St. Albans were too strong for the townsmen alone, he'd come along with 20,000 men and 'shave the monks' beards'.

There had been a long feud between abbey and town. The townsmen claimed that in far-off days, in the eighth century, King Offa had given them a charter, which had been stolen by the monks. As a result the abbot dominated everything and treated the people as his serfs. The merchants had no freedom to buy or sell—though some towns, built on royal demesne or belonging to a lay lord, had gained more independence already by the twelfth century than St. Albans had by the late fourteenth. Three times—in 1274, 1314, and 1326—the people had risen; but, after brief periods of freedom, had been put down again by the king. They had tried appealing to the law, but the law was the law of feudalism, and the decision always went to the abbot. The bitterest struggle was waged round the right to grind one's own corn. When the abbot won his case, he grabbed all the millstones of the citizens and paved his dining-room with them.

Grindcobbe, who had been brought up in the monastic school, had already been excommunicated and jailed for denouncing the monks, and the people wholeheartedly recognized him as their leader. After talking with Tyler he rode back the thirty miles without a halt and told the men of St. Albans of what had happened at Mile End, declaring that the King had given the people full right to act against the Abbot. The townsmen at once marched on the abbey and broke down the heavy gate to the Abbot's park. Next day they returned, drained the fishpond, killed the game, hacked down the hedges and removed all the emblems of privilege at which they had so long scowled. Land that had been seized by the Abbot was restored as commonland. The Abbot's jail was thrown open and the prisoners retried before a people's Court, which freed most of them; one prisoner, however, as a result of the retrial, was hanged. Then Grindcobbe's men arrived from London with the town's charter, and Grindcobbe arranged a meeting with the Abbot de la Mare. The Abbot put up a long fight, but, unable to deny the King's charter, he at last gave in. The abbey's charters were burned in the market-place, and the Abbot had to draw up and seal a charter granting the town its freedom.

Then the townsmen and the serfs presented their charters, and were given various rights by the Abbot: exemptions from tolls and dues, rights of pasturage on his wastelands, permission to hunt and fish in his woods and ponds, the right to grind their own corn and to elect a town government without interference. Similar charters had been granted to the men of Watford, Barnet, and Rickmansworth, who had aided St. Albans. The men of St. Albans further declared that they had as allies thirty-two other villages that, if called on, would come to their help.

But while these things were happening in Hertfordshire, the rebels were acting vigorously in London. After leaving Grindcobbe, Wat Tyler rode swiftly to the Tower with a strong detachment. On arrival, armed with the King's authority, he had little difficulty in entry. Indeed, no effort was made to defend or close the fortress. After the King had left, the drawbridge was not raised again, nor the portcullis lowered. The 600 men-at-arms guarding the stronghold made no resistance and the rebels treated them with all friendliness—stroking their beards shaking their hands, and saying that Tyler had no animosity towards them but had come to arrest traitors in the King's name.

The Tower. Temp. Henry VI.

The Queen Mother had come back to the Tower during the long negotiations at Mile End—probably after it had become clear that no violence would be offered to Richard and that he was carrying out his role of acquiescence with complete success. The rebels, breaking up into small bands, with Tyler and Farringdon at the head, ran through all the passages, climbed the narrow stairways, searched all the chambers, and even turned up the King's own bed to make sure that no traitors were hiding under it. They entered the Queen's room and engaged in some rough banter; one fellow is said even to have made an attempt to kiss her. She fainted and her pages were allowed to carry her off to a barge, in which she was rowed the short way to the Queen's Wardrobe near St. Paul's.

There was no difficulty in finding the wanted men. Sudbury, the Archbishop, had made one effort to slip away by boat; but a woman noticed him and raised the alarm. He hurried back to the Tower, and realizing that his end was near, had gone to the chapel. There he sang his Mass devoutly, confessed and gave communion to his colleague Hales. They went on waiting. Sudbury tried to fill the time in with services. He heard two Masses, or three, then chanted the commendations and the *placebo* and the *dirige* and the seven penitential psalms and the litany. He had reached the words '*Omnes sancti orate pro nobis*—all the saints, pray for us,' when the people burst in with a shout of triumph.

Brave at the last, he stood forward. 'Here am I, your Archbishop, no traitor nor soiler am I.' He stated that if he were put to death, the land would be laid under an interdiction.

Despite the deep religious feeling of the age, his words were greeted with shouts of laughter. The men replied that they were afraid neither of the Pope nor of his threats.

They seized him and dragged him out of the chapel, down the narrow stairs, across the green to the postern, then up to Tower Hill. There they lugged out a log of wood in place of the usual block; and the Archbishop, forgiving his enemies, was executed. The executioner, through incapacity or fear, took eight strokes to hack through his neck.

Next, the Treasurer Hales, then Legge and the King's confessor, Appledore, were executed. It is said also that a friar, the advisor of John of Gaunt, was caught and beheaded. All these men were executed by the rebels as traitors under the King's delegated authority; and they were killed quickly, without the refinements of drawing and quartering that were common in executions ordered by the King's judges. The heads of the slain men were then carried round the streets and set up on London Bridge, as was customary. To distinguish Sudbury, a mitre was put on his skull and fastened there with a nail.

It seems clear that when the King and the notables left the Tower for Mile End, they had abandoned Sudbury and Hales to the mercy of the rebels. If all the guards had gone off, the deserted ministers could have made an attempt to escape; but as Farringdon and his men remained keenly watching, they had no hope. Since Salisbury's plan of pretending to accept the peasants' programme had been accepted, there was no chance of saving the chancellor and the treasurer, and they were therefore cold-bloodedly deserted. After leaving Mile End, Richard and his retinue made no effort to regain the Tower. They went straight to the Wardrobe in Carter's Lane, by Ludgate Hill, and they must have previously decided on moving to that spot if their plans of lulling the minds of the peasants succeeded.

There was now no point in beleaguering the Tower. The main body of rebels therefore left that neighbourhood and went into the heart of the city. There were still many men at liberty whom they had condemned as enemies of the people. Farringdon was especially active in hunting such persons down. Alderman Horne patrolled the streets, asking if anyone wished to complain to him of any injury, and promising that 'he and his followers would quickly give them justice'. He compelled one man to pay a fine of £10 to a fishmonger, forced creditors to give their debtors bonds of release, and turned citizens out of houses to which he said they had no right—'thereby,' the indictment declared later, 'taking upon himself the royal prerogative of justice'.

Building a House.

Two more hated persons were arrested and executed. Wat himself is said to have taken Richard Lyons, the biggest and most ruthless speculator of all, with whom, as we saw, he seems to have had dealings in the French wars. The other man was Richard Imworth, chief jailer of the Marshalsea, well known for his merciless treatment of prisoners. A chronicler of the day states that 'he was a tormentor without pity', and if he could be so described in a period when all such jailers were brutal enough, he must indeed have been outstandingly callous.

Bands of rebels roamed about, stopping passers-by and asking them, 'With whom hold you?' If the man refused to say, 'With King Richard and the True Commons,' he was hustled to execution. This story is probably an exaggeration. All deaths were by beheading, and the men thus killed seem to have been all lawyers, jurymen of the city, officials connected with tax-levying, or recognized adherents of John of Gaunt.

In such a tumultuous situation there were no doubt mistakes made and private revenges worked out on a pretence of general justice. But certainly the intention of the rebels was to execute or molest only notorious oppressors of the people, and the leaders like Wat Tyler did their utmost to see that there were no disorders or perversions of the stated programme.

Hales's house at Highbury, we saw, was burned by Jack Straw. A band also went to destroy the house of the under-sheriff of Middlesex in the village of Knightsbridge. But another band with torches, which tried to enter the Guildhall and burn the documents and muniments there, was refused admission and made no further attempt to get in.

The one heavy blot on the proceedings was a movement to massacre the Flemings, some 150 or 160 of whom were executed. A man suspected of Flemish birth was asked to say 'Bread and cheese.' If he answered, 'Brod and case,' he was revealed as a Fleming. Houses of Lombard merchants and bankers from Italy were also attacked. The actions against the Flemings were wholly the work of London craftsmen, especially the weavers, who considered the Flemings to be unfair competitors and under-cutters. The assault on the Lombards must have been engineered by London merchants, their rivals.

Leaping through a Hoop.   (Ancient MS, engraved in Strutt's Sports.)

In a ring of about ten miles outside London, the villagers had risen, burned records and at times manors, and chased out unpopular landlords. There were strong outbreaks at Clapham, Croydon, Kennington, Kingston-on-Thames, Harrow, and Barnet. Men of almost every parish in Middlesex and north Surrey were later excluded from the general pardon issued by the King. Hendon, Hounslow, Ruislip, Twickenham, Chiswick, Carshalton, Sutton, Mitcham, and very many other places supplied their contingents of rebels, active locally or in London.

And all the while the tidings of hope were spreading yet farther out. In village streets and greens, along the roadways, at the door of alehouse or cottage, the people were talking. Messengers were galloping on sweaty horses through the summer days and nights; and where-ever they came, the people rose up and gathered at the customary place, an old oak or yew, a mound, a graveyard, a village cross. They collected their brown bows, their sickles and scythes, their knives, and waited, ready for the call.

CHAPTER 10

THE RISING SPREADS

ALL Saturday the 15th the people went on hunting out the men whom they had marked out as their enemies. But while they were thorough in tracking down their lesser opponents, they paid no attention to the point where the real threat lay. The nobles round the King were only biding their time. But the rebels do not seem to have set any guards round Carters Lane. Perhaps they thought that by showing a trust in the King they would bind him to them. But in fact their forbearance had the exact opposite effect. It emboldened Richard and his councillors to plan the undermining of the rebellion. At this moment Wat Tyler could easily have entered the Wardrobe with a strong force, arrested the nobles or sent them off to their estates, and ensured that the King was not used as a rallying-point against the charters of freedom. But he did not do so; and by his failure to take this crucial step, he doomed the rebellion and ensured his own speedy death.

All the while the clerks were at work by St. Paul's, turning out the charters; and men with these documents, which seemed to be precious titles of freedom, were hurrying out in all directions. They appeared in Cambridgeshire, Suffolk, Norfolk, Huntingdonshire, claiming to be members of a Great Society, an organization with definite political aims. Local leaders came conferring with Tyler, and returned home with deepened assurance.

In the north, the Midlands, and the west, as well as in parts of the south like Surrey and Sussex, there were risings of a sporadic kind, but no great movement. As the news from London came in, peasants burned manors, executed oppressors, and destroyed rolls or records. But mostly they were content with this local triumph and made no effort to link up with the main bodies of revolt. In any event, a large number of these outlying uprisings occurred after the rebels had been defeated in London.

Saying Grace.   (Royal MS. 14 E. 3.)

It was in East Anglia, a rich region, that a more serious and co-ordinated rebellion came about, on the same lines as those of Kent, Essex, and London. Here John Ball's preachings had spread wide and had struck home. The region was economically advanced, and there were many

F

striking contrasts. Some towns were free, while others were held back by the Church's conservative controls. Free labourers and freed serfs found themselves beside serfs and bound craftsmen. The Church authorities were particularly oppressive. The Church owned about a third of the land of England and was reluctant to give up any of its property-rights and to release its tenants from their services. Besides the enormous manorial estates, on which it enjoyed the profits of the lawcourts, it owned harbours and fisheries, forests and pastures, mines and markets.

Edward I and Edward III had already raised funds by confiscating alien priories; and shortly before Wat Tyler's revolt the reformer Wycliffe, supported by John of Gaunt, had begun to demand the general confiscation of the Church's wealth—a policy that was to be eventually carried out by Henry VIII in the sixteenth century. The programme of Tyler and Ball was far different, however, from Wycliffe's. Wycliffe wanted to share out the wealth among the impoverished gentry, who were then to govern the people justly. Ball and Tyler wanted the Church's lands to revert back to the peasants who worked them.

Among the East Anglian leaders were John Wrawe, a parochial chaplain, of Sudbury; Sir Roger Bacon, a landowner of Norfolk (and uncle of one of the Suffolk leaders, James de Bedingfield); Geoffrey Litster, a Norfolk dyer; Thomas, son of a knight, Thomas de Gyssing; John Chaevhevache; John de Montenay of Nokenham; and several tradesmen and merchants.

Wrawe had been in touch with Wat Tyler even before the entry into London. He left Tyler and rode through Essex to Liston in the north-west, where he found an

army already gathering—presumably the work of lieutenants whom he had left in the area. On 12 June, as
Tyler's captain, he took charge and sent messengers to
Sudbury, the neighbouring market town on the Suffolk
border across the Stour, calling on the citizens to join
him. Many of the men of Sudbury then marched to Liston
and Wrawe launched an attack on the manor house of
Overhall, which was owned by the hated Lyons. The
people burst in the doors and windows, and broke the
roof-tiles; and here, as everywhere, they burned the
records.

Next day Wrawe's force marched on to Cavendish
across the Suffolk border. Here lived Sir John Cavendish,
the Chief Justice, hated as a man who had been getting an
extra salary for enforcing the Statute of Labourers in Essex
and Suffolk; he was also chancellor of Cambridge University. He had hidden his valuables in the church belfry;
but Wrawe knew and had obtained the tower keys
through the aid of a Sudbury dyer. Cavendish's goods,
which included a velvet jacket worth 26s. 8d. and a silver
candlestick worth £7, were added to the war-chest.

The rebels then moved on to Milford Green where they
dined at a tavern, paying the fairly small sum of 3s. 4d.
Refreshed, they marched the seventeen miles to Bury St.
Edmunds, where the townsfolk had risen and were waiting for them before making an attack on the abbey. Now,
in the evening of the 13th, they met Wrawe's band at the
Southgate.

The abbey here was as detested as that at St. Albans,
and for the same reasons. There had been four previous
uprisings—in 1264, 1290, 1304, and 1337.

Early on the 14th the townsfolk, reinforced by Wrawe's

159

men, stormed the abbey and attacked the house of the prior, John de Cambridge. The prior was taken and sentenced to death by Wrawe. Wrawe meanwhile sent on to Thetford a small body of seventeen men under Geoffrey Parfay, vicar of All Souls, Sudbury, with his chaplain Thomas and Adam Bray, also of Sudbury. Parfay called together the mayor and chief citizens of Thetford and extracted forty marks of gold on threat of burning the town. The mayor at once agreed, and the money (less £4 that Parfay kept) was taken back to Wrawe.

Knights Combating. (Royal MS. 14 E. iii.)

About the same time, Cavendish, who had not been caught at his manor house, was hunted down. Seeing that his pursuers were catching him up, he made for the river Brandon, hoping perhaps to get away to Ely by the ferry. But Katherine Gamen of Lakenheath in the Fens recognized him and pushed the boat out into midstream. Arrested by John Pedder of Fordham, he was beheaded on the spot, and his head was carried back to Bury St. Edmunds, where it was set on the pillory with that of his friend, the prior. His house at Bury St. Edmunds was plundered, and a leader, Tavell, took his gilded sword.

The monks were forced by Wrawe to draw up a charter surrendering their claims on the town; and this, with deeds and muniments of abbey holdings, was handed to the citizens. The monks, as pledges that they would keep their word, were then forced to give up their jewels and holy relics.

For eight days Wrawe held the area. Some petty thefts were included in the later indictments; but generally the rebels acted with rigorous honesty. Wrawe sent out men to help other districts in revolt. Thus, Tavell and John Michel went into Cambridgeshire. They were dispatched to Ely, where the local rebels under William Combe were waiting for them. Combe had captured the bridge, which was kept open till Tavell and his troops rode through, then it was closed. Tavell and Michel took command. On Sunday, 16 June, an announcement was made from the pulpit in the monastery that proceedings in the King's name were to be taken against traitors. On Monday, the jail was stormed and the prisoners freed. A justice was tried and condemned.

Associated with the rebels were Geoffrey Cobbe, a man of considerable wealth, Robert Plumer, and Richard de Leyster, who did much in raising the countryside. Also, Thomas Wroo and Adam Clymme rode about, calling on the peasants. Clymme told them to stop all services to lords 'except as he, Adam, might inform them on behalf of the Great Society'. He also bade them execute everyone connected with the law and burn all documents.

At least two of the Cambridgeshire leaders had been in London with Wat Tyler. John Greyston fought with the men of Essex and Kent, then turned up at his home in Bottisham and led a rising there. John Stafford, saddler, had been living in London but returned home to help. By the 13th the Cambridgeshire rising was well under way and was spreading into Lincolnshire. Throughout, the actions were carried out in conjunction with Wrawe. His general command was accepted. It had been conferred, we may recall, by Tyler.

In Cambridge itself there had been an earlier rising in April. Now the mayor led an attack on the University and for three days he and his followers were in control. St. Mary's was taken and its large store of charters was burned in the market-place. The University authorities had to surrender their privileges and promise that for the future they would submit to the rulings of the town authorities.

A prior had enclosed the common pasturage. He was forced to sign a document in which he swore to pay over £2,000 if he ever prosecuted the townsfolk for what they had done against him.

Ship-building.

Wrawe had sent messengers also into Norfolk, where the people had gathered under the captaincy of Geoffrey Litster of Felmingham. Large-scale action was not, however, taken till the 17th. Litster, with Bacon as his lieutenant, seems to have been unknown to the authorities until he thus appeared as a leader of the people; but clearly the people themselves had known him well as a tried and resolute character. He was at once elected to the command and he firmly controlled the prosperous area from Cromer to Diss and Yarmouth. Attacks were made on manor houses and records were burned, but there were also attacks on foreign merchants who, by the use of cheap labour and the refusal to observe local customs, had attracted the hatred of both merchants and workers.

About a week before the rising, Litster had sent men riding round, to warn the groups in the various localities to hold themselves ready—another of the indications of a loose organization existing for some time before June 1381. Then, on 14 June, a proclamation was issued in Litster's name, calling on all men to assemble on Mousehold Heath above Norwich, a traditional meeting-place for rebels, which was to be used again in the great peasant rising under Robert Kett in 1549. By the 17th a host had gathered.

Litster opened negotiations with Sir Robert Salle, who had been chosen by the local gentry and the richer citizens to take command in Norwich. (Salle was the son of a stonemason, who had done well in the French wars and been knighted by Edward III.) 'Robert,' said Litster, 'you are a knight and a man of great weight in the country; renowned for your valour; yet notwithstanding all this, we know who you are; you are not a gentleman but the son of a poor mason, such as ourselves. Come with us.'

Salle did not like this reminder of his plebeian origin and he replied angrily. In the short fight that followed, he was killed. Norwich, a big trading and manufacturing centre with a large population, gave in as easily as London. The town authorities, scared at Salle's end, issued orders for the closure of the gates; but as the rebels neared, the craftsmen and poorer folk of the town demonstrated, and the city-fathers countermanded their orders. Some houses were burned, and a few 'traitors' (men who had administered the Stature of Labourers) were executed.

Fishing with a Seine Net.

Litster set up his headquarters in Norwich and sent men round to catch other such traitors, while Sir Roger Bacon was allotted the hard task of taking Yarmouth. This town, also a thriving place, was disliked by the rest of the county, since by one of its charters everyone living with seven miles of it had to buy and sell inside its bounds, and the lesser merchants both inside and outside the town had protested to Parliament against the extortions of the gild-members. Still, even Yarmouth welcomed the rebels and handed its charter over to Bacon, who tore it across and sent one half to Litster, one half to Wrawe. (Another charter gave Yarmouth the right to take tolls and interfere in the traffic to Lowestoft; and there was rivalry with London over the herring trade, as Yarmouth prevented the London fishmongers from gaining a complete monopoly.)

Here too some Flemings were executed—though surprisingly a Fleming, Richard Resch, was elected as the rebel leader of the town. Bacon took over the customs and appointed his own men as officers. He also set up a tribunal to deal with cases that had come up before or after the rising, and sent a petition to the King, asking for charters of freedom for his district on the lines agreed at Mile End and raising some particular points. The deputation consisted of three knights and three commoners.

Such details bring out the way in which everyone, apart from the nobility, now looked on the issues of the rebellion as settled, with the King fully acquiescing in the new system.

Risings kept on breaking out in an ever wider ring, at Winchester, Beverley, Scarborough, and so on. At Lincoln there were attacks on the Knights of St. John. There the leader was a priest, William Swepston, who gathered rebels from Dunsby and other estates of the Hospitallers.

At Bridgwater, Somerset, the leader was another priest, Nicholas Frampton, who had been in London and seen the execution of Sudbury and Hales. Delighted, he hurried back home, and with Thomas Engilby on 19 June he headed the attack on the Hospitallers, who were old enemies of the town. The master was forced to sign a document binding him to pay the town £200.

CHAPTER 11

DEATH AT
SMITHFIELD

From Carter's Lane the King's Council issued a proclamation that the people, having had their requests granted, were to leave London and proceed to their villages. Nobody took any notice, since now the Council had no authority. It is odd then that this effort by the Council to assert itself did not draw upon it the attention of Wat Tyler and John Ball. The fact that the Council thus continued to speak in the King's name and override the authority of Tyler was itself proof that the King and his councillors had not really accepted the situation brought about at Mile End, and should have been a warning that unless the Council was disbanded and the King taken into Tyler's council, there could be no security for the charters and concessions.

At the same time the King's councillors must have been much impressed and shaken by the abundant proofs that the peasants and craftsmen were perfectly capable of effective organization and of carrying on with the construction of a new social order. They must have discussed anxiously what had happened in France during the Jacquerie. Some of them must have been in that country during the violent peasant revolt. There they would have discussed the situation with the French nobles. Some of them may even have been present when Cale, the peasant leader, was invited to a conference with the French nobility for the discussion of terms. Cale was stabbed to death in the council chamber. (At the time there was a truce prevailing between England and France.) At least Salisbury, we may be sure, knew all about the murder of Cale and its effect on the French peasants.

Ordeal Combat or Duel. (Royal MS. 14 E. iii.)

Wat Tyler was the outstanding leader who had done most to build up a disciplined army in a few days out of the peasants and craftsmen. His authority was undisputed. We saw how even Bacon at Yarmouth sent half the torn charter to Wrawe at Bury St. Edmunds, and Wrawe had gained his strong position in East Anglia as the captain appointed by Tyler. The hopes of the rebels had more and more become concentrated in Tyler, to whom they looked as the man capable of standing up on their behalf before the King and the great men of the land. For any quick success of the royal cause, then, the elimination of Tyler was the first thing needed. Tyler must be murdered, as Cale had been.

He had been pressing for a further conference with the King. He wanted to carry out some more reforms. He could easily have announced these on his own authority, but he felt that it was necessary to have the King's consent. Salisbury and the other experienced nobles on the Council thus saw a chance of striking the blow which would make possible a turning of the tide of fortune.

There was no way, they knew, of luring Wat into a private conference where he could be conveniently removed as Cale had been. The murder would have to take place under much more difficult conditions. It would have to occur in the open, at some rendezvous with the rebel forces; and yet it must be veiled, hidden so that it would not be seen and understood at once by Tyler's followers. Otherwise the latter would be maddened into a wild retort that would mean the massacre of the whole Court, the King himself probably falling in the confused tumult.

There must then be no false step. Everything must be most carefully considered and worked out.

First, it was clear that soon, if nothing was done there would be no hope for their cause. They would remain alive, but they would lose their huge estates and the power that they derived from them. The King would pass over into the control of Tyler and Ball.

They therefore got into touch afresh with the bold

Furniture of a Bed-room of the time of Henry VI. (Harleian MS. 2278.)

mercenary, Sir Robert Knolles, against whose force the rebels had taken no action. They also sounded again the richer merchants and knights of London, working through their fervent supporter, the Lord Mayor. They saw that the time was now ripe to work on the fears of these citizens, many of whom might be pleased to see blows struck at John of Gaunt or at rival gilds, but none of whom would like a state of things in which the poor peasants and artisans were vocal and active. No doubt levies of a more systematic kind were being made for the purpose of feeding and lodging the host; and this also would cause discontent.

So by Saturday, the 15th, the Council had plucked up

its courage and gathered what support it could. Word was sent to Wat Tyler that the King would grant him audience in Smithfield at Vespers.

Richard and his retinue took a solemn farewell of their womenfolk. The King himself parted from the Queen Mother for the first time since the rebels had entered London. Clearly the action on which he and the courtiers were about to enter was considered uncertain and perilous. The party rode to Westminster, where they arrived about 3 o'clock in the afternoon. The monks came out with a cross. Richard dismounted, kissed the cross, and then, together with the others, knelt in prayer before the shrine and kissed the relics. He confessed and received absolution. There were loud and passionate prayers uttered. The knights, under their silken official robes of peace, wore coats of mail and carried swords. It was necessary for the rebels to think that they came without the means of fighting.

Now, if they had wished, they could have made a bid for freedom by riding off to Windsor Castle. But they must have had the feeling that everywhere they were surrounded by hostile peasants and that their only hope lay in bravely facing the danger and striking at its heart. At the same time they certainly felt that only luck and God's aid could make their plan succeed. It was more than likely that they would all be dead in a few hours.

Afternoon was drawing on as they set out for Smithfield. This area was then a wide open space outside the north walls of the city. Every Friday a cattle market was held there, with a fee of 1d. on the sale of every horse, every pair of oxen or cows, every four swine or eight sheep—the proceeds being applied to keeping the place clean. Yearly the great St. Bartholomew's Fair brought a huge and merry crowd on to the field; and now and then jousts were carried on there—as in October 1390, when sixty knights and sixty ladies rode from the Tower through Cheapside and the city to the green expanse, where twelve knights were ready to take the challenge of all stranger knights. One wonders how much Richard's thoughts turned then from the gay and courtly scene to the frightening June eve that he had spent there nine years before.

Tournament. The Melée. Thirty on each side. (Harleian MS. 4379.)

The courtiers now took up their positions between the Alders Gate and the Lud Gate, as far as possible from the rebel army, which was stationed near London Wall, deployed in battle order, with the two great standards and the banners granted by the King. Walworth rode out to call on Tyler to come forth and meet the King. The situation had been different at Mile End, when the King had humbly and unceremonially approached the rebels.

Wat Tyler, with one attendant carrying his banner, rode across to the King. He was clad in his ordinary clothes, armed only with a dagger. Why he came so unguarded is hard to explain. We can only surmise that the great success of the revolt, which seemed to have swept all opposition out of existence, had made the leaders lose all sense of proportion. They were behaving as if they were dealing with a broken power against which no precautions were necessary. And yet the very way in which the royal force was now confronting the rebel army should have shown that, so far from weakening, the King and his nobles were making a more compact show of opposition. But, instead of recognizing the new threat, Wat Tyler acted carelessly—as though, by reducing the occasion to a mere rendezvous between himself and Richard, he was stressing the fact that the people were now the sole power, with himself as their representative, and the King was a lesser force, no longer needing ceremonious treatment.

Nearing the King, Wat dismounted, dropped to one knee and took the King's hand, vigorously shaking it. He remarked heartily 'Brother, be of good cheer and joyful for you will soon have the Fifteenth pledged by the Commons more than you had before, and we shall be good comrades.'

He meant that the people would gladly pay the tax of a fifteenth to the King's exchequer and thus solve all his immediate problems of money. No doubt Richard looked white-faced and anxious, and Tyler blurted out this offer in order to cheer him up.

Richard then asked 'Why will you not go back to your own county?'—inferring that there was no reason for the people to stay under arms, since their demands had been met.

Tyler swore an oath that no one would leave till his further demands had been met; and he added, for the benefit of the listening lords, 'Much worse will it be for the lords of the realm if this charter be refused.'

Richard asked for details of the new demands.

Tyler read out the list. 'Let no law but the Law of Winchester prevail, and let no man be made outlaw by the decree of judged and lawyers. No man shall exercise lordship over the Commons; and since we are oppressed by so vast a horde of bishops and clerks, let there be but one bishop in England. The property and goods of the holy Church shall be taken and divided according to the needs of the people in each parish, after making provision for the existing clergy and monks, and finally let there be no more villeins in England, but all to be free and of one condition.' (One account adds that he also asked for the ending of the Game Laws.)

Playing Bears.

After he had set out his proposals in the name of the Commons of England, the King promptly agreed. 'All that you have asked for, I promise readily if only it be consistent with the regality of my crown. And now let the commons return home, since their requests have been granted.'

Richard could scarcely have understood all the implications of Tyler's demands; but he would feel clearly enough that they threatened the whole basis on which the feudal kingship depended. He however replied as the Council had decided he should reply. At this point there was to be no resistance made to anything that Tyler said.

What exactly were the implications of the demands? First, the proposal that only the Law of Winchester should prevail had very important consequences. That Statute, passed under Edward I, had represented an effort to cut down feudal disorder and its effects of violence and arbitrary action. By it the highways leading to market-towns were to be made wider with a space of 200 feet on either side kept clear of all bushes and obstructions. The responsibility for keeping the roadsides open was put on the manor lords. The people were to be responsible for the maintenance of law and order in their own area: that is, the freemen who had the right to bear arms were to become the main force for ensuring that the King's law was carried out and obeyed. But, as we saw earlier, the Statute of Labourers, with other ordinances aimed at keeping the peasants tied down and at ensuring a supply of cheap labour, had necessitated a considerable increase of the apparatus of the State. Such laws had speeded up the growth of the central power and the machinery needed to enforce its decisions. They had brought about the appointment of new officials, new bodies of administrators and agents of the law, such as the tax-collectors.

All this meant a development in the opposite direction to that suggested by the Law of Winchester. Instead of the legal system being based in the people, it was ever more compactly based in officials, justices of the peace, and so on. No other way could the Statute of Labourers have been enforced. If the lords had had to appeal to the freemen of a locality to arrest and terrify the unwilling peasants and labourers, they could have done nothing.

So, in asking that the Law of Winchester be made the basis of the legal system, the rebels were asking for a reversal of the whole tendency of law and administration since Edward I. No doubt they felt that they were appealing to an ancient customary democracy; and though this democracy had never existed in the terms in which they visualized it, the appeal was none the less potent and had its roots in a genuine tradition. Since, under their scheme of things, all serfs became free, the law in their reorganization would be administered by the people as a whole, in their own interests.

The second proposal—that the sentence of outlawry should no longer be pronounced against anyone—had the same sort of aims in view as the first one. Outlawry meant the deprivation of all legal rights, of all property, and all the forms that normally protected a man. Once a man condemned to outlawry could be killed on sight with impunity. Now that could no longer be done; but the crushing nature of the sentence remained. And under the Statute of Labourers it had been increasingly used to overawe the peasants and labourers. Any serf or labourer who fled to escape the effects of the Statute was out-lawed after 1360; and when captured, he was sent back to the manor from which he had fled. There he was branded on the brow with the letter F (for Flight).

Penny of Richard II.

With such penalties threatening the peasant, there could be no secure freedom. On the other hand, if the Law of Winchester were effectively carried out, the people themselves would determine the ways in which the new system was applied, and would no longer feel that the law was a weapon to be used against them.

The rebels had already demanded the abolition of serf-dom, and Richard had agreed to the demand at Mile End. But this point was so central in the whole pro-gramme of the rebels that they rightly felt it could not be too often repeated. Here it was once more brought in to make clear how they conceived the future working of the Law of Winchester.

To make sure that the point would be grasped, they added the highly important demand that every man should be responsible only to the law of the King. This meant that the whole system of complicated feudal courts put-ting the peasants (or even the townsmen in such cases as Bury St. Edmunds and St. Albans) at the mercy of the manor lords would be wiped out.

They now brought in the question of the organization of the Church, to complete the picture. In their scheme,

176

the clergy were to be paid a sufficient wage, but all the rest of the vast wealth of the Church was to go to raising the standard of living of the people as a whole. The rebels were in no way opposed to the village priest, who was close to the people. Many such priests not only supported the rebellion, but also played an active part in it. What the rebels wanted was to end the great political power of the Church as well as to break down its economic grip on so many sections of the nation. By proposing one bishop they wanted to end the complicated system of ranks and powers inside the Church.

Tyler had put the demands so concisely that probably none of the lords who heard him speak could have understood what a shattering effect they would have had on the feudal order. Like Richard, they would merely feel a general threat as well as an incredible insolence in a rank commoner daring to talk about systems of government at all.

Wat felt the strain. His throat was dry. He called for water to clear the dust from his mouth. He rinsed out his mouth and spat. Then he drank a large draught of ale—a sort of toast to the new order which he felt had been brought into being by the King's ready acceptance of the new demands. To the lords such behaviour was an intolerable rudeness on the part of a commoner, a final touch to the whole insolence of the scene.

Finishing the ale, Wat mounted his horse to ride back to his army with the great tidings of a new world.

But at once the King's retinue moved forward and surrounded him. He was cut off from his own men. In the gathering dusk the rebel host could not see at all clearly what was happening. Now became plain the reasons for the Council in choosing so late an hour of the day for the meeting, and so broad a space as Smithfields.

Out of the closing ring of knights and lords, a young page, following his orders, cried that he knew this Wat Tyler, who was the greatest thief and robber in the whole of Kent. Apparently, because Wat had come at the head of the Kentish army, the Court thought him a Kentishman, though in fact he was of Essex.

Tyler was angry, but remained calm. He asked that the defamer should come out and face him, for he was now the King's chief counsellor and not lightly to be insulted.

The lad stayed where he was, and went on jeering, using harsher terms.

Tyler again demanded that the accuser should come out and confront him; and this time the courtiers thrust the lad forward. He repeated his charges, apologized for arguing in front of the King, and repeated that he spoke the truth. He said that he did not deserve the death that Tyler was now demanding.

So far Tyler had been careful to give no pretext for the courtiers to draw their swords. But the tension of the situation began to tell on him. He had been worked up to a high pitch of excitement by presenting himself before the King with the demands which he felt would create a new and free England. He had relaxed in rinsing his mouth out and drinking the ale; and now the courtiers were buzzing round with hornet-insults. As they pressed in closer, he took out his dagger, perhaps to strike at the mocking page boy, more likely to protect himself from the danger that had become obvious.

This was what they had all been waiting for. The whole provocation had been aimed at driving him to lose his self-control and make a gesture that could be interpreted as violent.

Walworth at once charged forward, crying that he'd arrest anyone who drew a weapon in the King's presence. Wat Tyler struck back at him, but a dagger was useless against the breastplate hidden under the mayor's robes. Walworth struck twice, at Wat's head and neck. Wat fell back wounded. Then all the courtiers came rushing in, wildly striking and slashing. Ralph Standish and John Cavendish hacked away at him as he lay helpless on his horse. What happened to Wat's attendant we are not told. We may assume that he was either cut down or was hustled aside and arrested.

Quarter-staff. (From the old Ballad of Robin Hood and the Tanner.)

Wat made one more effort. He spurred his horse and broke away, desperately turning towards his army. But the horse had gone only fourscore paces when, succumbing to his wounds, he fell off.

The army did not know what had happened. In the owl-light of the dusk they saw only some vague movements among the King's retinue. Then they saw a horseman, apparently Tyler, breaking away from the crowd of knights; and they suspected foul play. Shouting with rage, they prepared for action.

But before any orders could be given for attack by the uncertain officers—before a flight of arrows could begin the annihilation of the royal party—Richard now carried out the last part of the Council's scheme. What he had to do was by far more difficult than any of the actions so far done; and it is unlikely that, boy as he was, he would have had the bold initiative to ride forward and address the rebels unless Salisbury and the others had schooled him in the steps to be taken. In any event, he had the courage to spur his horse on and to call out a few but essential words to pacify the rebels.

'Tyler has been knighted,' he cried. 'Your demands have been granted.'

He added that the army was to march to St. John's Fields in Clerkenwell, where Tyler would be waiting for them.

Obeying the King, in whom they trusted, they marched off to the Fields. Richard quickly slipped away in another direction with some retainers and was conducted through the city by Walworth. The other courtiers, following the agreed plan, had ridden straight off to London, to collect and lead the various groups of royalists who had been secretly mustering throughout the day in the twenty-four wards.

However, the two rebel aldermen, Sybyle and Horne, had witnessed the slaying of Tyler from the city walls. They made a last attempt to save the situation. Riding through Aldersgate to Westcheap, they sounded the alarm.

'Citizens, shut your gates and put a guard upon the walls, otherwise all is lost!'

Another version says that, to rally the citizens, they rode about, shouting that the King had been slain and so everyone should ignore appeals to march to his aid. Whatever they did, they were too late. They managed to close the Aldersgate, but could not prevent the Mayor's forces from gathering to threaten the rebels. These forces now consisted of mercenaries, the retainers of various lords, rich merchants and their followers, with other citizens who had grown alarmed at the growing power of the common folk. There was much confusion, and no doubt some of the men now rallying to Walworth and Richard came rushing out at the cry that the rebels were killing the King. Anyhow, one way and another, a large royalist body emerged from the wards, led by Knolles, Brembre, Philpot, and others of the King's retinue. And so, by the time the rebel host had arrived at St. John's Fields, the royalists were able to surge from the North-west Gate and surround them.

The fact that they were ready for action in so short a time and that they had known where to go is the final proof that the whole affair of Smithfield, the provocation and killing of Wat Tyler together with the King's speech directing the host to St. John's Fields, had all been part of a carefully prearranged plan.

Walworth, after escorting the King through the city to the Fields, returned to Smithfield. He was taking no chances about Wat Tyler, whom he detested. He expected to find the dead or dying body of the man still lying on the ground; but a few rebels, who must have been dissatisfied with the King's explanations and orders, had stayed behind to look over the darkened field. They found the body and carried it off, grieving, to St. Bartholomew's Hospital near by. Tyler was not yet quite dead. He was put in the master's chamber. Walworth pushed his way in, dragged the dying man out of bed, along the ground and into the middle of Smithfield. There he cut off Tyler's head and stuck it on his lance. With the head triumphantly held aloft, he rode back to the King.

Genoese Archer, winding up or bending his Cross-bow.

When he arrived on the Fields with Tyler's bleeding head on his lance, the rebels were thrown into extreme perplexity and despair. By this time night must have fallen, and they stood there in a vast darkness, with torches flaring around them. They had marched with the hope of seeing their commander greet them in the splendour of newly-gained honours; instead they saw his gory head brandished in triumph. During their march, rumours must have circulated and apprehensions must have grown. With no one to come forward with an immediate and bold call to action, they felt lost and betrayed. With cries of dismay they sank to their knees in the wheat-fields.

The lords wanted to rush in and massacre them. But Knolles and Salisbury held them back. They pointed out that the men were still armed. An attack might well en-rage them and restore their courage; and then, even if the King's forces won, the victory would be a costly one. Further, there were still considerable rebel forces inside London—men who for one reason or another had not marched to Smithfield—and in the counties the rebellion was now only getting fully under way. The only sensible course was to proceed with caution. Above all, now as at the beginning, the essential thing was to get the peasants dispersed. Then revenge would be easy and cheap.

Salisbury had his way. An announcement was made that the commoners, with all their aims won, should now return home. The disheartened peasants, still cherishing the belief that the charters and concessions would be honoured, agreed at last to disperse. Headed by two knights, they let themselves be taken through London and then be sent off on their various ways.

Their cause was lost.

Richard rode back to his mother. 'Ah, fair son,' she said, 'what pain and anguish have I had for you this day.'

He replied, 'Certes, madame, I know it well. But now rejoice and praise God, for today I have recovered my heritage that was lost, and the realm of England also.'

Certainly, though the scheme which won the day was the work of Salisbury and his like, Richard had shown much courage in riding forward to address the rebels. It was the high moment of his career as a king. Henceforth he was to show a mixture of incapacity and instability that led to his deposition by Henry Bolingbroke, and to his own murder.

CHAPTER 12

THE END OF IT ALL

ONE striking fact is the lack of leadership shown among the rebels as soon as Tyler was struck down. Yet the story of the revolt shows no lack of strong characters ready to take the initiative in their own hands. We must infer that Tyler and his council in London had badly overestimated the apathy and confusion among the courtiers. The rebels had been lulled into a sense of false security and had seen in the Smithfield rendezvous only a repetition of what had happened at Mile End. The active leaders must have all been absent on what they thought were more important matters. The King's assent to the Smithfield demands was of course essential to the success of the revolt, but they must have considered that it was a foregone conclusion, a mere matter of routine, which could be left to Wat Tyler alone.

Otherwise it is hard to see why he went over to the King's party unaccompanied by his lieutenants. If John Ball, Jack Straw, Farringdon and others had been with him, the scheme of murder could not have been carried out so smoothly and the rebel army could not have been confused and deceived.

We must therefore assume that the leaders who could have stepped at an emergency into Tyler's shoes were all absent from Smithfield and St. John's Fields; and this fact made possible the complete success of Salisbury's plan.

As the crestfallen rebels moved away from St. John's Fields, the King called Walworth, Brembre, and Philpot, and knighted them. London was put in their charge, with Knolles to aid them; they were given the power to execute and mutilate as they wished. Bands of mercenaries at once went through London, murdering and cutting down people on all sides. Scores of rebels were haled to the block in Cheapside and beheaded. Anyone looking like a peasant was in danger. Some rebels were handed over to the relatives of the slain Flemings, who were told to take any revenge on them they liked.

Several of the rebel leaders were caught and executed without trial. These included John Kerby, Alan Threder, Jack Straw. It seems that they and others had stayed on in London when the army marched out to Smithfield, carrying on with the work of organizing the revolt and dealing with the messengers that were continually coming in from the outer shires.

Jack Straw, of whom we know nothing but the tradition that he was a priest like John Ball, was considered important enough to be held for interrogation by Walworth. The latter hoped to draw from him details of the rebel organization and evidence incriminating others. He promised to have Masses said for his soul for three years if he made a full confession of the rebels' schemes.

They stood there, the exultant mayor whose plans had all come true, and the defeated peasant-priest. Around them, in the wild fiery night, the clash of weapons sounded, the cries of hunted men, of men caught and struck down in some dark alley where their blood would clot on the cobbles, the shouts of soldiers as they dragged some wretch up to the watchfires.

Fire-bell Gate (and Curfew), Barking, Essex.

Jack Straw betrayed no one; but in his moment of defeat, with death looming up near, he spoke of the plans that had heartened himself and his fellows in their tremendous venture. According to the account taken down and recorded, he declared that Tyler meant to keep the King as hostage and carry him off through the shires, using the royal name as a cloak to all his actions. He meant to arrest and execute the great magnates, and to seize all Church property. The rebels intended to make an end altogether of bishops, canons, rectors, abbots, and monks, but were going to respect the mendicant friars. Finally Tyler meant to execute the King himself, 'and when there was no one greater or stronger or more learned than ourselves surviving, we would have made such laws as pleased us'. Tyler would have governed Kent and set his lieutenants over other counties. If the King had not surrendered at Smithfield, London would have been fired that night and the rich houses sacked.

On the whole the statement rings true, though it looks as if the scribes gave it a tone as horrifying as possible for men of a feudal mind; they may well have done so without meaning any distortion, since they and their masters could not at all enter into the minds and motives of Tyler and his followers. They could only see such men as a destructive horde like a plague of locusts, an elemental fury like a terrific storm. But if we allow for this inevitable exaggeration and distortion, as in the threat to fire London—which Tyler would certainly not have done, since it would have reduced many thousands of his followers to destitution and misery, and would have scared the other towns—there is nothing in what Jack Straw is stated to have said that runs counter to the programme as set out at Mile End and Smithfield.

Probably Tyler had said that if the King did not truly fall in with the new order, he would have to be executed. What is most interesting in Jack Straw's statement, however, is the plan it reveals to abolish the monarchy and to decentralize England, to break it up into a number of separate districts under leaders acclaimed or appointed by the people. Here again we see how much thought had been given by the rebel leaders to the sort of society which they wanted to see emerge from the changes they hoped to bring about.

Another rebel executed by Walworth's court-martial

was John Sterling, an Essex man, who said that he had cut off Salisbury's head. He had drawn attention to himself by going about with a drawn sword hanging down in front of his neck and a dagger dangling down his back. Till the end he went on glorying in the part he had played in executing the Archbishop.

As soon as London had been secured, the King's Council turned to deal with the counties. They sent out urgent calls to all the lords in the near areas to rally to the royal standard set up on Blackheath. The lords and their men gathered there, coming out from the woodlands and other hiding-places where they had been lurking, from the barricaded manor houses or the keeps of castles.

By the 18th a sufficiently large force had gathered for the King's Council to feel able to proclaim the arrest of all malefactors and the dispersal of all unruly groups. The Blackheath army was divided into companies, each of which was allotted an area to control. The main body, under the King, rode into Essex, where the people still maintained that their acts had been royally approved and were therefore legal, and that they themselves were ready to stand by their rights.

On 22 June this body entered Waltham, where Richard set up his standard. A deputation from the large rebel forces awaited him with demands for the ratification of the charters he had granted. They also asked for all the rights that were now due to them as free men.

In their reply the Council let loose all their long pent-up fury through the mouth of the King: 'O most vile and odious by land and sea, you who are not worthy to live when compared with the lords whom you have attacked; you should be forthwith punished with vilest deaths were it not for the office you bear. Go back to your comrades and bear the King's answer. You were and are serfs, and shall remain in bondage, not that of old, but in one infinitely worse, more vile without comparison. For as long as we live, and by God's help rule over this realm, we shall attempt by all our faculties, power and means to make you such an example of offence to the heirs of your servitude as that they may have you before their eyes as in a mirror, and you may supply them with a perpetual ground for cursing and fearing you, and fear to commit the like.'

The Council also issued a proclamation stating that the King in no way sympathized with the cause of the rebels and that the peasants must not use his name to cover up their crimes. This proclamation brings out the deep extent to which, in the face of all evidence to the contrary, the peasants still clung pathetically to the belief that the King was really on their side—that he had only been misled by bad men.

The deputation reported back to the peasant army at Billericay. The men declared that they'd enjoy the freedom they had won or die in its defence. They sent for reinforcements, which came from Great Baddow and Rettenden. Then they built strong defensive positions in the woods, with the flanks guarded by ditches and by carts chained together. All this was in the usual vein of the day's tactics.

The Council then dispatched a large force of heavy armed cavalry and men-at-arms, the vanguard of the royal army. This force arrived at the Billericay positions on 28 June, and a fierce fight developed. But the palisades were stormed by a horse charge and the rebels retreated,

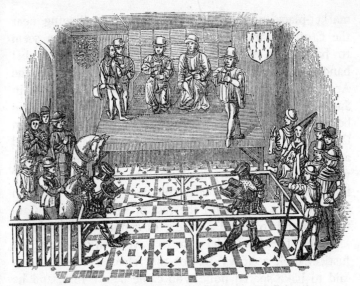

Tilting-match between Nich. Clifford and J. Boucmell. (From Froissart.)

leaving 500 dead, but with intact formations, to Colchester and to Huntingdon, where they tried to rouse the people. But their appeal was in vain. The people had lost heart.

The rebels then marched to Sudbury in an effort to join forces with Wrawe. There they found that he had already been defeated and that they had to face fresh troops. There was another pitched batle, but now the odds were weighted against them. Many were killed, others hunted and cut down in thickets, or captured. Some escaped and for a while there were isolated risings in various parts of the county. Earlier, another band had marched to Guildford, where they made a stand but were beaten.

The battle of Sudbury seems to have been fought in the

market-place, and in the 1930's workmen digging near the Croft unearthed many headless bodies. These seem to have been those of beheaded peasants. The rebel band must have somehow carried off the head of the Archbishop Simon Sudbury; for that head still remains in Sudbury town, in the Church of St. Gregory. Simon had been a benefactor of his home place. He helped John Colney to found a Leper Hospital by the Melford Road and the friars of the Priory to lay a conduit of fresh water across the Stour; he also helped to rebuild a part of the church where his head still lies (with only a lump of lead in its stead with the rest of his remains at Canterbury) and to found a college of canons and chaplains.

Robert Tressilian, successor to Cavendish as Lord Chief Justice, took a heavy toll of the rebels. For long he is said to have spared none who came before him, and he sentenced so many at a time that nine or ten men had to hang on a single beam. (He was himself convicted of treason seven years later and hunted down in the gutter of a Westminster house; he was found to wear under his clothes a large number of charms with signs painted on them like the Zodiac, one with a demon's head, others with the names of demons. He believed that he could not die while he was draped with these things.) When he and the King arrived together at Chelmsford, Richard issued a proclamation revoking all the charters he had granted and withdrawing all his pledges. The rebels did not cringe or beg for mercy, but went to their death as they had fought.

At St. Albans, Grindcobbe had tried to rally the people when the news came that the King was marching against them. 'Be of good heart, for we are well provided. Help will not be wanting for us, as long as our money shall not fail. See, the towns around us are in alliance with us, and they will come to our help if need be. Let us ride forth tomorrow like men, to meet the knights outside the town, and let us ask, before they get near to our town, whether their coming is in peace. And if not, we will drive them from our town with blows.'

The people were encouraged and rode out to meet the attackers. But they found only Sir Walter Atte Lee, who came from the area and who had told the King that he could arrest Grindcobbe without any battle being fought. The knight harangued the people and said he came as a friend. He advised them to surrender, as the King was coming with so huge an army that 'for miles around no fodder nor any corn, no fruits of the earth, fresh or old, are left, but all things are consumed or trodden under'. After thus working up the fears of his listeners that their farmlands would be wrecked, he advised them, 'as a neighbour and friend', to deliver up their leaders to him and restore to the Abbot all they had taken from him, including the charters.

He ended by choosing twelve men and empanelling them as a jury for the indictment of the ringleaders of the revolt. Their reply, however, was of little use to him. They said that 'they could indict none, could charge none; that all were good and faithful men of the King and they knew none else amongst them'. They considered that all actions had been carried out according to the King's will.

Walter Atte Lee now resolved to use force. Covertly summoning some bailiffs and retainers of the Abbot, he bade them arrest the three chief leaders in the dead of night and carry them off at once to Hertford, where he would be waiting.

The arrests were successfully made. When the citizens found what had happened, they had recourse again to arms. They sent some of their most important men to Hertford to ask for Grindcobbe's liberation. He was let go, under the pledge that he must use his influence on the Abbot's side; and the delegates were told that unless the charters were given back, he would be beheaded.

Bob-Apple.

The people then insisted that the charters must be returned and Grindcobbe saved. He refused to accept this offer. He told the assembled townsfolk, 'Fellow citizens, your newborn liberty has at last removed the burden of an age-old tyranny. Stand firm while you may. Lose no courage because of the penalty to be inflicted on me. I am to die for that liberty which we have won. But if I fall, I shall think myself happy to end my life as a martyr for such a cause. Act now as you would have acted had my head been struck off in Hertford yesterday.'

The men of St. Albans swore to defend their freedom. They regretted that they had not executed Atte Lee while they had the chance. But now Tressilian and his troops entered the town. Tressilian cheated a reluctant jury into indicting Grindcobbe and others by telling them falsely that another jury had already done so; and to prove his claim, he showed them indictments which in fact dealt with other cases.

Grindcobbe and fifteen others were hanged and drawn. The King issued a special order that they were to hang on the gibbet 'for as long as they should last'. But the people cut the bodies down and gave them secret burial. The graves, however, were traced and the King commanded the bodies to be exhumed and hanged again on the gibbet.

An even more important prisoner than Grindcobbe was brought before Tressilian at St. Albans. John Ball had been arrested at Coventry. He may have gone there from London after the defeat at St. John's Fields, or he may have been already outside London on some missionary or organizing work. In any event, the fact that he was arrested at Coventry suggests that he was not present in the army that marched to Smithfield.

He was brought to trial on 13 July. Some of his letters or messages calling for the revolt were read. Without hesitation he avowed his authorship, proudly acknowledged his part in the struggle, and declared that he had no regrets. He refused to ask pardon of the King and was sentenced to be hanged, drawn, and quartered—that is, to have his entrails taken out while he was half-strangled and his body hacked into four bits, which would be sent out to different danger-points and nailed there as warnings.

His execution, however, was delayed for two days at the request of the Bishop of London, who hoped that in the interval Ball would repent. He did not repent and was executed on the 15th, his dismembered body being sent to the four corners of England to be exposed as a warning to the commoners.

Criminals conducted to Prison. (Harleian MS. No. 4374.)

On the 16th John Shirle was arrested at Cambridge. He was one of the messengers who claimed to belong to the Great Society. He had evaded capture, but the news of Ball's arrest was too much for him. He held a meeting in a Cambridge tavern where he told a large body of listeners what Ball had stood for. He declared that Richard and his ministers should have been the ones with their heads on the block, and he prophesied that Ball would soon be avenged.

On trial he did not deny his words but went defiant to his death. Two others, John Wright and George Dunsby, charged with taking messages of revolt through Norfolk, also declared, as they went to the scaffold, their pride in having been able to serve the Commons faithfully.

The East Anglian rising was crushed by the Bishop of Norwich, Henry Spencer, a fighting man who, however, recalled his priestly role by often confessing men before putting them to death. A monk cried, 'To those who were killed in battle, the Bishop's sword brought absolution.' He had championed Pope Urban in the period when there were two rival popes, and had been granted power to absolve of all sins, not only of the living, but also of their ancestors. The chronicler Knighton states, 'It was told how certain of his commissaries asserted that, at their command, angels came down from heaven and snatched from their pains the souls that lay in purgatory, and brought them straightway to heaven.' However, the Bishop had backed the wrong pope, and after helping to slaughter some 3,000 of the opposing side, he returned home a defeated man. Now he took out on the peasants any chagrin he still felt.

He rode with his two-handed sword from Peterborough to Ramsey, then on to Cambridge and Newmarket. Near Icklingham he met the men sent by Litster to the King for further charters. He questioned the knights, hanged the peasants, and freed the others. Then he rode on to Norwich. Litster had left the town and made his stand at North Walsham. The Bishop, as soon as he sighted the enemy, ordered a cavalry charge, which he himself led. The heavily-armed knights and men-at-arms broke through the defences and slaughtered all they could catch. The Bishop, in his killing, 'foamed at the mouth like a wild boar'.

197

G*

Litster, captured, was tried by the Bishop, who confessed and absolved as well as condemned him. Then, as Litster was being dragged to the gallows on a hurdle, the Bishop raised the condemned man's head so that it would not be bruised on the stones of the road. A quarter of the mangled body was sent to be nailed on the house which had been his headquarters at Norwich. The other quarters went to Harwich, Yarmouth, and Lynn.

As far as we know, John Wrawe was the only leader who turned King's evidence at his trial and agreed to draw up a list indicting all who had joined with him. However, he gained nothing by his cowardice and was hanged in June 1382.

The rebels in Kent fought on as hard as those in Essex and East Anglia. For three months the county was still restive. At the end of August the Earl of Kent (who had slipped away during the ride to Mile End) had a look at the villages and reported that the King and his Council could safely visit the area. Richard came and inspected the corpses hanging from the gallows.

Then on 29 September rebellion broke out again. A large force captured Maidstone, arrested the sheriff and some others of the gentry, and put them to death. They then marched to Deptford. Demanding the ratification of their charters, they threatened the King and his Court with death if their request was denied. Here, as in Shirle's speech in the Cambridge tavern, we see that the people had at last lost faith in the King.

Still, they found it hard to imagine a country without its king; and according to one man, Cole, they were thinking of setting up John of Gaunt in Richard's place. Gaunt, as we have seen, had all along been especially hated. But through his absence he had taken no part in the deception and the repressing of the peasants; and so, in the recoil against Richard, some of the Kentish rebels seem to have thought of him more kindly.

Criminals conducted to Death.   (Harleian MS. No. 4374.)

After the first wholesale killings and hangings, the proceedings of the King and his Council were not harsh by medieval standards. Most of the rich or well-born men who had joined the rebels were jailed, but not executed. Even the rowdy Farringdon, after a long-drawn process of law, was issued with letters of grace on 8 March 1382. Sybyle, Carlyll, and Tonge were let go on sureties of £300 each, fifteen days after Easter 1383, as the Court could not find enough evidence against them. They had refused to benefit by an amnesty of November 1381, as to appeal to it would have implied a recognition of their guilt; and in 1384, through lack of witnesses, they were finally acquitted. Sir Roger Bacon was a short while in the Tower, then freed, while Robert Cave, baker of Deptford, being a poor commoner, was sentenced to ten years' jail. As conditions in prison were extremely foul and prisoners were often dependent on charity to a considerable extent for food, such a sentence came near to one of lingering death.

Also, apart from the reprisals taken during the suppression of the revolt, everyone was tried by jury and no extensive search was made for the rank-and-file rebels. The number of pardons was quite unusual.

The reasons for this forebearance did not however lie in any humane attitude. The rebellion had been very widespread and had deep roots. It was by no means thoroughly crushed, as we see from the September rising in Kent. Further, in 1382 there was another broadly-based plot in Norfolk to kill the Bishop of Norwich in return for Litster's death. The conspirators planned to descend on the people gathered at Faiths Fair, rush them into an oath to rise in the name of the True Commons, and make the marshgirt abbey of St. Benet's-at-Holme their headquarters. Two years later another design for rising in Norfolk in support of the programme of Ball and Tyler was discovered.

In 1383 a crowd in Sussex stormed Lewes Castle and burned all the rolls, rentals, and charters of its owner, the Earl of Arundel. The same year had a rising at Hollesley in east Suffolk which lasted three days and saw the sacking of several houses. An insurrection broke out in 1392-3 affecting Cheshire and West Yorkshire—areas that had not had time to rise at Tyler's call.

In London the conflict of Victuallers and Clothiers flared up immediately after Tyler's death. Street battles went on in 1382-3 when the Mayor was a champion of the Commons and advocated cheap food. Another outburst came in 1393, so that the King deposed the Mayor and appointed a military governor for the city for several months.

Similar disorders continued through the fifteenth century Norwich was up in arms four times between 1433 and 1444, and there was much tumult in the affairs of Exeter, Bristol, and Lincoln. In 1450 came the great uprising of the Commons under Jack Cade, in which the grievances covered a much wider social range than had the comparatively simple anti-feudal demands of Ball and Tyler. In 1549, as part of a wide movement of unrest, East Anglia rose under Robert Kett and the people held Norwich.

Further, a movement of religious reform, led by Wycliffe, had only just begun when the peasants rose in 1381. Wycliffe's Poor Preachers had already gone out, though they played no part in the bringing about of the revolt. Still, after 1381 the Government was increasingly concerned about the agitation of Wycliffe's followers, the Lollards, who represented an early manifestation of the forces which matured into the Reformation of the sixteenth century.

There was thus abundant reason for the King's Council to decide that the best policy was to let sleeping dogs lie and not to stir up more resistance. Even more important, perhaps, was the fact that they could not afford to kill off large numbers of peasants. As we saw, a main factor of all the troubles lay in the shortage of labour which the Black Death had rendered more acute. Wantonly to increase the shortage would be to cause the lords more troubles than they wanted—troubles that would not be compensated by any feelings of satisfied revenge.

And so the Government acted circumspectly and liberally by medieval standards.

A general pardon was proclaimed by Parliament on 13 November 1381—a pardon which however excluded 287 of the leaders and the more insurgent of the towns. Not for some time did Bury St. Edmunds, Cambridge, Scarborough, Bridgwater, and others find themselves treated as normal law-abiding places.

Funeral of Richard II. (Illumination in Froissart.)

CHAPTER 13

AFTERMATH

———————

THE Commons—the True Commons, as they called themselves—had suffered a heavy defeat. Despite all the troubles and riots that followed, the burden of serfdom had been legally once more rivetted on large sections of the peasantry. But that does not mean that the whole thing had been futile.

The revolt was an inevitable expression of the decay of feudalism. If we look at western Europe as a whole, we see that it was part of a widespread movement against feudal obstructions. The Commons of Florence rose in 1378, and the weavers of Ghent and Bruges in 1379-82. Thus, in parts of the Continent where textiles were highly developed, something of the same sort of crisis had set in as in the advanced areas of England.

Such movements played their part in breaking down feudalism, in intensifying its inner crisis, and in speeding up its decay. They thus brought nearer the day when the aims of rebels of 1381, at least in large part, would be realized—that is, when serfdom would be wiped out and markets freed.

On a long-distance view we can say that there were two aspects of the situation in 1381 that were largely to determine England's future in making her the first great industrial country. These were the growth of rich farmers in the villagers and the system of 'putting-out' manufactures from the towns. The rich farmers chafed against the lords' restrictions and wanted to play an ever bigger part in the markets; the merchants at the head of gilds like those of the Clothworkers, Drapers, Leathersellers, Cordwainers, Cutlers, and Pewterers, who invested their money in the handicraft industries of the countryside, were playing an important part in breaking down the restrictions that ruled in the town. The two groups slowly came together and played essential roles in building the cloth manufactures which did so much to establish England's industrial position.

The Husbandmen haunting the King's dreams. Vision of Henry II.

We may say, however, that Tyler's revolt was doomed from the outset because, however strong and capable the leaders the peasants might throw up, they could not themselves take over political power. They were accustomed to organization in small communities struggling hard to survive with relatively primitive agricultural techniques. Their groups were also unstable in the sense that, with the growing money-economy, a few of the members were rising up towards the level of the gentry, while others were sinking lower down into landless penury.

If they had grasped Richard while it was still in their power, they could not have restored the small free communities of which they dreamed—communities in which everyone was more or less equal, with a small but prosperous farm. If they had really broken the manor lords, power would have shifted to the merchant and the money-lender—often the same person.

They expressed their weakness by their hope that some how the King would sympathize with their dream and come out on their side—so that there would somehow be a government ensuring their small prosperous and equal communities, but in no way interfering with them.

But this element of illusion in their hopes does not make their programme any the less remarkable, any the less far-seeing in certain respects. They were right in realizing that serfdom belonged to an outworn age and must end. They were right in seeing that the King's law must be extended and that the private law courts of the lords must go. They were right in seeing that the way forward lay through the markets being made free of all the feudal restrictions and controls.

And there was a deep element of love and of respect for man as man, for the dignity of man, in the doctrines of John Ball, to which they passionately responded—something which could not then be carried into practice, but which held at its core all the democratic rights and aspirations that have since been gained or can ever be gained.

The crisis in the feudal system continued through the fifteenth century. The differences in status among the peasantry went on increasing, and the richer peasants took part in the domestic production of woollens, in which England was coming to lead Europe. In domestic production, the goods were made at home by peasant craftsmen, with the merchant organizing things and making good profits, free from the gild-controls of the towns. More and more cropland was enclosed so that it might pasture sheep and produce wool for the manufacturers; and large numbers of villages were destroyed and peasants evicted. (This was one of the prime causes of Kett's rebellion.)

The defeat of the peasants in 1381 opened the way to the deepening of rivalries among the great nobles and

Parliament assembled for the Deposition of Richard II.

thus to the civil wars that kept on breaking out, after the deposition and murder of Richard II, throughout the fifteenth century. Richard's end came in 1399 through his cousin, the son of John of Gaunt. After long strife the Yorkist faction won in 1461, but was then overthrown by the Tudor branch of the House of Lancaster in 1485. The Tudors brought about a considerable increase in the centralization of power, drawing together the various feudal rights and privileges in the Crown's hands. This centralization, carried on by the Stuarts, in time led to conflicts with the class of country gentry and merchants which wanted freedom to develop industry and trade in their own way. Hence the Cromwellian revolution that came about in the 1640's and broke down the final forms of the feudal State.

Cromwell thus completed what Wat Tyler had begun. But the national situation had greatly changed in the intervening 260 years, and so the aims of the rebels had changed considerably. However, there was an element of continuity as well as of difference, and among the poorer classes the ideas of what was needed had not changed so very much from those of John Ball and Wat Tyler in their broader aspects. 1381, 1450, 1549 had shown a rising challenge from the common folk to the feudal order, which came to a decisive head in the 1640's. Tyler, Cade, Kett, and Oliver Cromwell all belonged to a single tradition in many aspects.

Meanwhile, the pressures of trade and industry had slowly but powerfully broken down the system of serfdom which Richard and his Council had announced as eternally fixed on the peasants. The leasing of demesne land, or the turning of it into pasturage, went on steadily, and there was less and less profit to be got out of enforcing the old feudal burdens of serfdom. The serfs faded out. They became landless labourers or took over land as lease-holders, with their servitudes commuted to money pay-ments. We find serfdom mentioned in 1529 as an out-dated nuisance that still lingered on in parts, and Elizabeth I found a few villeins on the royal demesne whom she freed in 1574. But, in effect, by the time the Tudors came to the throne, serfdom had ceased to play an important part in English society.

Though, then, the revolt of 1381 did not at all directly bring about the conditions at which it aimed, it was a powerful factor in the medley of forces expressing and increasing the decay of the feudal system. From one angle, it seems a bitter and tragic expression of hopes and aspirations that came to total disaster; from another, it reveals the undaunted forces in the common folk who, despite everything, went on hoping and working for a better world, and it therefore had its element of victory at the heart of its defeat.

It was a great moment, one of those when suddenly the deep forces of humanity show themselves in a situa-tion that seems dark with cruelty and oppression. True, the rebel peasants and craftsmen were guilty of much violence and many deaths. But when we consider what they had suffered, we are surprised rather at the high degree of order in their actions and the way in which they sought (apart from the murders of the Flemings) to act in what seemed to them a constitutional way against only their inveterate enemies. They felt the need to destroy these men, not so much out of revenge for the things they had done, as to clear the way and ensure that the new England would not fall back into the old ways of corruption and oppression.

Though Wat Tyler comes up into the light of history for only a few days, he stands out clearly. A rough and hearty character, he had great powers of organization

Coronation of Henry IV. (Harleian MS. No. 4679.)

and could attract the devotion of the large numbers of peasants and craftsmen who served under his captaincy. In the glimpses we get through John Ball's sermons, Tyler's programme of political demands, and Jack Straw's gallows-statement, we gain a fascinating glimpse of the minds of these commoners, about whom, in normal times, the medieval writers of history maintained a contemptuous silence. We see that Tyler was capable of bold views of society and history, that he could conceive radical reforms, and that he could work out a comprehensive and unified picture of what he felt to be a worthy society in which men could freely achieve the good life.

For these reasons he deserves a high place among the heroes of England's history, among the men who have expressed and formed her national character and traditions. The days when he had control as the virtual ruler of England came to be known among the common folk as the Hurling Time. Hurling was an ancient ball-game of the hockey kind. The days of Wat Tyler were thus remembered as a time of universal festivity, when life had suddenly become a tense and stirring game of opposed sides, with the old burdens thrown away. A game in which only the real qualities of a man mattered, not his place in the social system.

BATTERSEA
PUBLIC
LIBRARIES

NOTE ON BOOKS FOR FURTHER READING

There are four books in English that deal directly with the Revolt. These are: *The Great Revolt* by Sir C. Oman, *The Rising in East Anglia in 1381* by E. Powell, *The Peasants' Revolt of 1381* by P. Lindsay and R. Groves, and *The English Rising of 1381* by H. Fagan and R. H. Hilton. All are worth reading. The bias of Oman is against the Peasants. The book by Fagan and Hilton has an excellent account of the background, and its reconstruction of the events at Smithfield is the most convincing. Important also are Studies in the Sources of the Social Revolt in 1381 by G. Kriehn in the *American Historical Review* (vii 254-85, 458-85), and Hilton's account of pre-1381 peasant movements in England in the *Economic History Review* of 1949. Naturally the episode comes into all historical works dealing with England of the 14th century, such as A. Steele's *Richard II*.

Valuable source-books, giving contemporary documents, are *Illustrations of Chaucer's England* by D. Hughes, *The Peasants' Rising and the Lollards* by E. Powell and G. M. Trevelyan, *Chaucer's World* by E. Rickert, and *Social Life in Britain from the Conquest to the Reformation* by C. G. Coulton. Other interesting works are *Chaucer and his England* by Coulton, *Social Life in the Days of Piers Plowman* by D. Chadwick, *Life in an Old English Town* by M. D. Harris. For the crucial development of Textiles there are E. Power's *Medieval English Wool Trade* and *Medieval People*. As general works there are D. M. Stenton's *English Society in the Early Middle Ages*, A. R. Myers' *England in the Later Middle Ages* (both in the Pelican History of England), and G. O. Sayles' *The Medieval Foundations of England*. More detailed bibliographies will be found in many of these works. The Penguin *Atlas of Medieval History*, edited by C. McEvedy, will help for the general European background.

However, anyone interested in the period must turn to the poems of Chaucer and to Langland's *Piers Plowman* (modernised version in Everyman Library).

INDEX

215

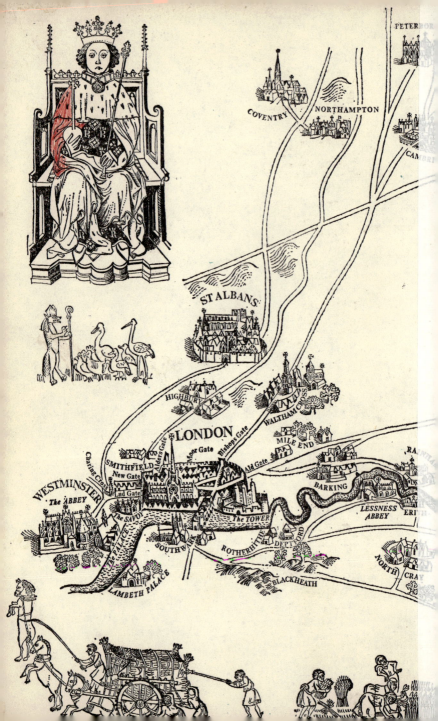

PETERBOR

COVENTRY   NORTHAMPTON

CAMBRI

CA

ST ALBANS

HIGHBURY

WALTHAM C

LONDON

Bishops Gate

MILE END

Moor Gate

RA   N   A

Aldersgate

SMITHFIELD

Ald Gate

New Gate

Lud Gate

BARKING

Charing Cross

WESTMINSTER

LESSNESS
ABBEY

ERITH

The ABBEY

The SAVOY

The TOWER

The PALACE

SOUTHWARK

ROTHERHITHE

DEPTFORD

NORTH

CRAY

LAMBETH PALACE

BLACKHEATH